The Complete Guide to
Robert's Rules of Order
Made Easy

Everything You Need to Know Explained Simply

By Rita Cook

THE COMPLETE GUIDE TO ROBERT'S RULES OF ORDER MADE EASY: EVERYTHING YOU NEED TO KNOW EXPLAINED SIMPLY

Copyright © 2008 by Atlantic Publishing Group, Inc.
1405 SW 6th Ave. • Ocala, Florida 34471 • 800-814-1132 • 352-622-1875–Fax
Web site: www.atlantic-pub.com • E-mail: sales@atlantic-pub.com
SAN Number: 268-1250

ISBN-13: 978-1-60138-259-7   ISBN-10: 1-60138-259-6

Library of Congress Cataloging-in-Publication Data

Cook, Rita, 1964-
 The complete guide to Robert's rules of order made easy : everything you need to know explained simply / by Rita Cook.
    p. cm.
Includes bibliographical references and index.
ISBN-13: 978-1-60138-259-7 (alk. paper)
ISBN-10: 1-60138-259-6 (alk. paper)
1. Robert, Henry M. (Henry Martyn), 1837-1923. Robert's rules of order. 2. Parliamentary practice. I. Title.

JF515.R66C66 2008
060.4'2--dc22
          2008030283

INTERIOR LAYOUT DESIGN: Nicole Deck ndeck@atlantic-pub.com

Printed in the United States

# Dedication

This book is dedicated to my husband, Russell William Dandridge.

We recently lost our beloved pet "Bear," who was not only our best and dearest friend, but also the "Vice President of Sunshine" here at Atlantic Publishing. He did not receive a salary but worked tirelessly 24 hours a day to please his parents. Bear was a rescue dog that turned around and showered myself, my wife Sherri, his grandparents Jean, Bob and Nancy and every person and animal he met (maybe not rabbits) with friendship and love. He made a lot of people smile every day.

We wanted you to know that a portion of the profits of this book will be donated to The Humane Society of the United States.

— *Douglas & Sherri Brown*

THE HUMANE SOCIETY
OF THE UNITED STATES ©

The human-animal bond is as old as human history. We cherish our animal companions for their unconditional affection and acceptance. We feel a thrill when we glimpse wild creatures in their natural habitat or in our own backyard.

Unfortunately, the human-animal bond has at times been weakened. Humans have exploited some animal species to the point of extinction.

The Humane Society of the United States makes a difference in the lives of animals here at home and worldwide. The HSUS is dedicated to creating a world where our relationship with animals is guided by compassion. We seek a truly humane society in which animals are respected for their intrinsic value, and where the human-animal bond is strong.

Want to help animals? We have plenty of suggestions. Adopt a pet from a local shelter, or join The Humane Society and be a part of our work to help companion animals and wildlife. You will be funding our educational, legislative, investigative and outreach projects in the United States and across the globe.

Or perhaps you'd like to make a memorial donation in honor of a pet, friend or relative? You can through our Kindred Spirits program. And if you'd like to contribute in a more structured way, our Planned Giving Office has suggestions about estate planning, annuities, and even gifts of stock that avoid capital gains taxes.

Maybe you have land that you would like to preserve as a lasting habitat for wildlife. Our Wildlife Land Trust can help you. Perhaps the land you want to share is a backyard — that's enough. Our Urban Wildlife Sanctuary Program will show you how to create a habitat for your wild neighbors.

So you see, it's easy to help animals. And The HSUS is here to help.

The Humane Society of the United States
2100 L Street NW
Washington, DC 20037
202-452-1100
www.hsus.org

Table of Contents

# Introduction

Robert's Rules of Order: you have most likely heard the term used if you have ever taken part in a formal meeting. Most people are too embarrassed to say, "What are Robert's Rules of Order?" so this book will explain it to you in easy-to-understand language, and you will never have to ask.

The first chapter will cover this more in detail, but "Robert" was a person, General Henry Martyn Robert, and these rules are named after him. He got involved in what is known as parliamentary procedure when he began presiding at meetings and did not know all of the rules involved.

"My embarrassment was supreme," it is noted that he said. "I plunged in, trusting to Providence that the Assembly would behave itself."

People who especially have a need to know Robert's Rules of Order include chairmen of boards, politicians, and higher-ups in corporations. With these rules in place, professionals have the ability to run meetings with ease. The most important thing to remember when leading a meeting is to stay in control of it. How do you do that? Robert's Rules of Order.

Other key position holders in meetings who use Robert's Rules of Order are secretaries and treasurers. These positions are present in government meetings such as city councils.

Robert's Rules of Order have been edited over the years, and the manual is now in its Tenth Edition. Even so, the rules are still difficult to understand without some help.

Indeed, there are many books that have been written on Robert's Rules of Order, but many are just too long and tedious to get through. For the person who needs the information fast, "just the facts" essentially, this book, *The Complete Guide to Robert's Rules of Order Made Easy: Everything You Need to Know Explained Simply* will be your best tool. After all, if you are in a position to run a meeting that requires Robert's Rules of Order, you likely cannot remember every in-depth passage that is written explaining the rules.

Also in this book is information you will need for running an electronic meeting. Indeed, in today's world, executives live all over the world and increasingly travel; it is not always possible to get everyone in the same room at the same time. Robert's Rules of Order can still be used no matter how many different parts of the world your coworkers and colleagues are located in during the meeting.

Every meeting, no matter what the company or organization, will get the best results by using Robert's Rules of Order. These rules require structure and a business-like approach to situations. It is all about majority making the decision but the minority of people still being heard.

Handy definitions of many words you will encounter in this book and when discussing Robert's Rules of Order with others can be found at the end of this book.

# Chapter 1
The History of Robert's Rules of Order

The Rise of Democracy as a Form of Government

"The people" define democracy, as opposed to other forms of government, as government. However, a true democracy would require that all members of the group vote on all actions of the group (or society). Therefore, logistics make a true democracy nearly impossible except in small groups. To this end, the form of democracy most familiar in the modern world is what is called a "representative democracy." This type of democracy employs elections to create a group of representatives who will then make the decisions on behalf of the whole body. This type of governance is not new, though, and has been around since before recorded history. You might be surprised to learn that the ancient Israelites of the Bible used a religious-based representative democracy. Representatives of the 12 tribes made decisions, dating back to as early as the wanderings in the desert with Moses.

In the Americas, the native tribes that now make up the Northeastern states also used a democratic form of government to organize their various tribes into one nation.

Today, many of the laws and practices that we use come from a defined and written code of conduct that was used in the Republic of Rome where participation in the public forum was considered the mark of manhood.

In England, democratic forms of government were common among the tribes who lived in and were native to that island. After the Anglo-Saxon invasion in the 5th century, the monarchy was established and became the ruling form of government, with the reagent's power being derived from a witenagemot, also defined as an Anglo-Saxon advisory council to the king. The witenagemot was created with 100 nobles, prelates, and other important people who took part in the administration on an ongoing basis. With the Norman conquest of England, the government of the land was formalized and the Great Council was formed to unite the various factions and barons under one central government. During this time, the land was administered using a feudal system in which a king was understood to own all the land, and local barons, on swearing fealty to that king, were given a piece of the kingdom to administer.

Local farmers grew crops and sustained themselves through this means. They were permitted to work the land in return for swearing fealty to the barons (and also the king). This gave the nobility a percentage of the workers' harvest, and in return for these oaths of fealty, the nobility provided protection and administration for the land and kingdom. To organize and authorize protection actions, such as declaring war or removing a fellow baron who was not doing his job, the barons came together to have discussions with each other. These Great Councils morphed into a parliament when King Henry III called the Great Council together to discuss not only his business, but also any concerns about the management of the lands.

Originally, there existed only the House of Lords, which was made up of landed nobility (persons associated with the royal household who actually owned the land) and which was empowered to make decisions for the government of those lands as a whole. Later, the House of Commons, composed of representatives elected by the common people, was added to give the non-nobility a voice in the decision making process.

Parliamentary Procedure

In short, parliamentary procedure makes up the rules that are used to conduct meetings of any kind. Anyone can use these procedures, but not everyone necessarily needs to. It depends on the meeting, the group, and the situation. The group using the procedures might be called a deliberative assembly, and an organized system of making decisions needs to be in place. Parliamentary procedure is a respectful way for everyone to be heard and for meetings to run as smoothly as possible.

For the most part, this type of procedure is used by all governing bodies who operate constitutionally, government or otherwise. Common sense is key in figuring out how to make these practices work, but it is duly noted that these procedures protect everyone involved in the meeting. Parliamentary procedure should be an asset, not a stumbling block, and Robert himself said, "The assembly meets to transact business, not to have members exploit their knowledge of parliamentary law."

The development of Rules of Order, which would become the foundation of parliamentary procedure, came about because of a drawn-out internal fight within the English Parliament during the 16th and 17th centuries. Before this time, customs and traditions had been the primary governance in how business was conducted within the body. In varying attempts to handle the conversation, resulting disagreements gave rise to a body of writing on the procedures to be used in the House of Commons. These rules, called common parliamentary law, came to North America with the original colonists. Conversely, because the parliamentary law was being written even as the colonists immigrated to the New World, their knowledge and understanding of these regulations was incomplete.

Even with incomplete, or rather unfinished, knowledge of parliamentary law, though, the colonists still knew the importance of understanding how a deliberative assembly, such as a parliament or an organization, conducted business. These colonists' lives and livelihoods were based on the individual charters granted to them by their home countries. Companies in their home countries that operated on a for-profit basis owned many of these charters. Once in the New World, the colonists set about creating their own rules and governance. As each colony varied in its charter and customs, so did the resulting rules regarding the procedure of conducting an assembly.

When the colonies rebelled against the English government, it was for the most part concerning the way in which they were being allowed (or rather not allowed) to participate in the representative democracy to which they were required to swear fealty and provide taxes. The revolutionary cry "No taxation without representation" refers to the need of the colonies to be represented in the British Parliament on an equal scale with their fellow countrymen back home. When this failed to create change, their solution was a revolution and the establishment of a new state.

After the Revolutionary War, the Continental Congress worked to develop a constitution and system of government that would provide representation to all the persons while also allowing for efficient management of the country. In the development of the Senate, the Continental Congress drew heavily on the example of the British two-house system of parliament.

Early Precursors to Robert's Rules

When Thomas Jefferson presided in the Senate as the vice president, he gained an understanding of how diverse the traditions of government were among the various statesmen. As the presiding officer in the Senate, Jefferson was called on to make rulings on matters of procedure and process that had not yet been clearly defined. Beginning with a few notes, Jefferson went on to create a book of rules to govern the Senate proceedings for his term and later presiding officers. In the years that followed, Jefferson's publication of the *Manual of Parliamentary Practice* became the standard for the operations of governmental bodies, although it was still a bit unwieldy for volunteer and civic organizations.

As the new country grew, so did a new culture and new society. People formed business groups, welfare organizations, and political bodies. The need for standard rules to govern the growing number of these societies and groups became apparent. In response to this need, Luther S. Cushing developed a manual that was well received but that left much of the day-to-day functioning for individual assemblies open. Cushing believed that each assembly should develop its own rules of order to govern its activities, and his book was accordingly geared only to regularly accepted customs and practices. It was thought that this would give individual assemblies autonomy and independence. Unfortunately, the task of developing cohesive rules of order proved beyond the capabilities or inclinations of most assemblies.

Who is Robert?

Enter Robert. Henry Martyn Robert was an engineer and eventually a general, and he developed these rules in 1870. Robert gained his first interest in parliamentary procedure when he was unexpectedly called on to lead a church meeting yet had no idea how to do it properly. Recently transferred to New Bedford, Massachusetts, Robert found himself in an awfully embarrassing situation in his attempt to lead the assembly. Without any knowledge of what he was doing, he vowed to learn about parliamentary procedure before he would ever again find himself in such a position. After some research, he found a few books that had some basic rules for legislative assemblies. Carrying these with him on a card, he was at least a little better prepared the next time.

When he and his wife were later transferred to San Francisco, California, they became active members of the community and participated in different organizations locally and from around the country. Once again, Henry Robert found that his rules were not sufficient to the task laid before them. He found that the rules he had learned were not only insufficient, they were also not universally accepted, which caused no end of tension and friction among the societies he was involved in on a regular basis. After further research and growing concern for the societies in which he was involved, he created a pamphlet of rules for these organizations. These pamphlets were well received by the organizations that he was a member of, but he was never able to truly finish the task.

After another transfer, Robert found himself moved again to the study of parliamentary procedures. Having studied Cushing's manual by this time, Robert became convinced that Cushing's approach needed revising. Instead of a few broad rules that allowed societies to establish their individual codes of conduct, what was needed was a basic manual that, once learned, would enable a person to move from one society to another with relative ease and understanding. Being deeply convicted of this need, he set about writing a book of rules that would address this problem. This book, which became wildly popular, is what we have come to know as *Robert's Rules*.

Basic Principles of Robert's Rules

The point of Robert's Rules is to provide support for the rights of many different groups, thereby making sure the majority vote rules but that everyone is heard. Robert's Rules protect the rights of the majority to prevent a tyranny and also prevent corrupt rule by one person. Anarchy, the opposite of tyranny but the corrupt rule of the masses, is also protected against in Robert's Rules, with protection of the rights of the dissenting minority. The goal is to ensure that the minority has a chance to say its case and, failing to convert the majority, the opportunity to acquiesce gracefully. Robert's Rules also protect the rights of individual members, giving them the right to voice their support or dissension equally. Finally, Robert's Rules protect those who are absent from the assembly and ultimately protects the rights of the deliberative society as a whole.

The basics of these rules are fairly easy to understand, with there being ten main points that make up the bigger picture.

1   The privileges of the entire group are more important than the privileges of the members on an individual basis.

2.   Everyone is equal (that is good democracy and really, the only democracy).

3.   A certain number of voting members must be present in order for votes to be made legal. If there is a question, this information is normally listed in the bylaws as to what makes up a group's quorum.

4.   The majority vote wins the day.

5.   If you decide not to vote, then you are making the decision to go along with the majority vote.

6.   The two-third vote is not always used, but it needs to be incorporated when a vote is being taken to change something already in existence.

7.   Members who are given the floor to speak should be treated with respect and not interrupted.

8.   Motions must be debated as long as members want it, unless a two-thirds vote makes the motion undebatable at any given point.

9.   Once a motion is made and voted on, a member cannot bring it up again for vote in the same meeting.

10. Never take things personally.

These days, *Robert's Rules of Order* is in its tenth edition, this last one being published in 2000. Below is a list of the ten revisions with some explanation and year of publication.

- **First edition**, published in 1876 — The actual title of the first edition book was known as the *Pocket Manual of Rules of Order for Deliberative Assemblies*. Robert himself had these published, but only a total of 4,000, and they sold out in less than a year.

- **Second edition**, published in 1876 — Robert made a few changes and sold these after the success of his first book earlier in the year.

- **Third edition**, published in 1893 — Again, Robert made changes to this edition based on feedback he received from his two earlier editions.

- **Fourth edition**, published in 1915 — Robert made more revisions for this edition and named it officially *Robert's Rules of Order Revised*. He noted that many people had contacted him regarding sections that needed revision and expounding, so this was considered his bigger and better version.

- **Fifth edition**, published in 1943 — Although Robert died 20 years before this edition came out, this 1943 fifth edition incorporates notes that he made before his death.

- **Sixth edition**, published in 1951 — This was the 75th Anniversary Edition.

- **Seventh edition**, published 1970 — This edition turned out to be about 594 pages and doubled what existed before. It was called *Robert's Rules of Order Newly Revised*, and it included examples and explanations of the rules. It was revised by the wife of Henry's son with some additional help as well.

- **Eighth edition**, published in 1981 — Minor changes that did not make much of a difference to the book at all.

- **Ninth edition**, published in 1990 — This new edition ended up being 706 pages long, with many changes.

The notable changes are also discussed in the preface of the book.

- **Tenth edition**, published in 2000 — This edition is mostly the same as the ninth, but it also updates information. Again, for information on the changes, you can find it in the preface of the new book.

Chapter 2
Robert's Rules for Your Organization

Determining if You Need Them

Before you propose that your group of friends adopt Robert's Rules for your decision making process on where to go for dinner, it is important to understand the types of organizations where Robert's Rules work best. A "deliberative assembly" is the type of gathering that is frequently understood as needing and using parliamentary law, most likely not what you would call you and your group of friends trying to decide on dinner plans. A deliberative assembly is the type of group that needs some way of organizing and conducting its business. Use the following list to help you answer that question:

- Is your group meeting to decide what type of action the group should take as a whole?

- Is the group meeting in such a way that all members can communicate with each other simultaneously?

- Is the group more than 12 people (other rules apply for fewer than 12 people)?

- Are all members free to act according to their own judgment?

- Are all your members equal in their rights to determine the actions of the group?

- Is it all right if someone disagrees?

- Can those present make a decision for the whole group, including anyone not present at the time of the decision making process?

Using these questions, look again at our example of your group of friends deciding where to go for dinner. Yes, you are meeting to make a decision for the actions of the group. Yes, you are all standing around the office talking about where you should go for dinner. Yes, you have 14 people going to dinner. Yes, all members can make their own decisions, which means no one is a slave or beholden to any of the other members of the group. Yes, everyone can have an equal vote, and yes it is all right if someone disagrees. However, this is where things get sticky. Chances are that someone will be allergic to some type of food or unable to afford a specific type of restaurant. If one disagrees with the vote of the whole group for these reasons, he or she may not be able to go to dinner with everyone. Also, if someone is coming to dinner but not at the office, he or she might not want to have a decision made for him or her. Most important, it would almost certainly be unwieldy to adopt Robert's Rules formally for such a decision.

The main division is that if you and a group of friends are deciding where to go for dinner, you in all probability do not need to adopt Robert's Rules to make the decision. If you are a group of friends in a club for the promotion of widgets, you might need them. If you are a group of friends who happen to own the controlling stock of a Fortune 500 company, you undoubtedly need them.

What Robert's Rules of Order Can Do For Your Group

When determining whether to use Robert's Rules of Order, think about the advantages and disadvantages of using these procedures. You can expect your meetings to be shorter, more formal, legal, and, most important, inclusive — everyone's voice will be heard.

- Robert's Rules will help keep meetings on track and to the point. The good thing about meetings that are run succinctly means they are short, and you do not spend all night debating an issue or arguing a point. Robert's Rules limit the time that a person can speak (ten minutes) and how many times that person can speak (no more than two) on any given issue. No rambling either; whatever motion is on the floor for discussion is the only topic to be discussed at that time.

- You can expect meetings in which you get more done. When you have particular items to discuss, you can make your points and move on. This allows time for more topics of discussion.

- You will likely find less bickering. Indeed, the meeting will be more formal, even among friends. The good news is that when two people do not agree, they will still respect each other when the meeting is over.

- There will be less chance of your being sued when using Robert's Rules of Order. When you use Robert's Rules of Order, you are following proper governing rules and keeping documents to avoid litigation.

- Everyone gets a voice, and that makes the rules even more effective for the present and the future. The one thing to remember when voting, though, is that you should know what your bylaws say about a quorum. Regarding the winning of a majority vote, there must be a quorum present to vote, and if the bylaws do not outline the definition, then it is more often than not said to be the majority of the membership.

Charters

Many groups that you will be involved with are local or regional branches of a larger organization, or parent organization. Parent organizations have, as part of their charters and bylaws, a predetermined organizational structure for their local branches. If you are establishing a new local branch, you need to check with your parent group for organizational documents such as charters and bylaws.

If your organization is a new or unique one, it will be up to the founding group to create a charter, bylaws, and file Articles of Incorporation when necessary. It is recommended that all organizations establish charters; organizations that are seeking to do financial business, whether for profit or not, are required by state law to have a written charter. In most of these cases, the charter or purpose is part of the articles of incorporation required by the state to create your organization. Consult with an attorney for the creation of any necessary paperwork.

Even if you are not planning on doing financial business, you should still consider writing a charter. A charter creates the course that the organization will take. It is where the vision and the mission of the assembly are defined and articulated for the rest of the world to know. This document is the foundation for your organization's operations, and it provides the foundational principles by which the society will operate. For example, the charter for the Leukemia and Lymphoma Society is what specifies the work the society does to raise money and search for cures to these diseases. This organization's charter defines that it will be raising money for leukemia and not planting inner-city gardens. Bylaws and constitutions, which define the organizational structure, can be similar in many organizations, but the charter for every organization should be unique. In essence, a written charter sets the mission of your newly created deliberative assembly.

Bylaws and Constitutions

If a charter sets the mission of the organization, the bylaws or the constitution create the organizational principles by which that deliberative assembly will go about achieving this mission. The recommendation of parliamentarians is more often than not that bylaws be used to include the traditional elements of a constitution instead of creating two separate documents. The bylaws of an organization define the structure of the organization and the particulars of operation, including everything from the pay for CEOs to the mode of communication by which your meetings will be held. Robert's Rules provide an outline of the basic bylaw articles needed, which are as follows:

1. **Name** — The full name of your organization, including punctuation. In most cases this explains who you are and what you stand for.

2. **Object** — A brief statement, in general terms, of the object of the society and its various aspects. It gives the person who does not understand your group a quick overview of what to expect.

3. **Members** — This should consist of sections that include: the classes of members, membership eligibility, fees and dues, duties and rights of members, resignation, and honorary members, with definitions for better understanding.

4. **Officers** — These should be listed by rank and should include at least the president and secretary and also the methods of nominating and electing members, term limits, and any duties that are different from those outlined by the parliamentary authority.

5. **Meetings** — This section will list information on the regular, annual, and special meetings, including how they are called, what consists of a quorum, and how to change a meeting in the case of an emergency.

6. **Executive Board** — The establishment of a board whose members are the officers of the organization and whose powers and rules are then defined herein.

These board members might also have meetings that are closed but are for the good of the membership.

7. **Committees** — This section defines the establishment of standing committees and their composition and duties. Also, there should be provisions for the establishment of special committees.

8. **Parliamentary Authority** — This addresses the rules of order that the organization will use to conduct its business and the rights assigned to members. Many times, this section will be the place where the organization will itemize the use of Robert's Rules as its parliamentary authority.

9. **Amendments** — This is where the bylaws are outlined and may be changed should the group see the need to do so.

Additionally, you may choose to include information to items pertaining to:

- Finances

- Nominations and elections

- Local or national organizational affiliations

- Fees or dues

Rules of Order

Any deliberative assembly needs rules and guidelines as to how it will conduct business. As covered in Chapter 1, there are many different ways of organizing your society and establishing practices for deliberation. Though, normally, there are three different ways to determine your rules of order.

1. **Create your own rules** of order. This is not recommended. The creation of and adoption of a completely new set of rules of order is a long and arduous task.

2. **Use an existing set** of rules, with Robert's Rules of Order being the standard. This is the easiest and most efficient way to establish a parliamentary procedure for your organization.

3. **Combine the use of Robert's Rules** with rules written specifically for the organization and its purposes. This is the most common and most flexible way to effectively use rules of order that are appropriate to your organization. In this case, Robert's Rules would be your fundamental rule of order, and the bylaws would enumerate specific additional or alternative rules that are appropriate for your organization.

If no rule of order was incorporated into the original bylaws of your organization at the time the bylaws were written, using the method for amending the bylaws gives the organization the tools it needs to choose a rule of order to operate by in the future. This is most frequently found in an organization that grew organically and did not have a formal starting or when the bare minimum was included in the bylaws for incorporation concerns.

We Have Adopted Robert's Rules... Now What?

Once the deliberative assembly has formally adopted Robert's Rules as its rules of order, it is necessary to immediately undertake the task of educating all the members in the understanding of the rules. The National Association of Parliamentarians (**http://parliamentarians. org/grouplearning.php**) has many resources that can assist in this process, from pamphlets to introductory books that provide a basic understanding of how to use Robert's Rules. It is important that the leadership of the organization be familiar with the use of parliamentary procedure and that the body be educated in it so that there will be no confusion when the Rules are truly being used.

Look at the various kinds of meetings that you can hold with Robert's Rules of Order in place, after adopting them for your organization. A meeting, according to Robert's Rules, is defined as a group of people belonging to an organization who meet to conduct business. If the meeting is more than one meeting, like a convention, that is called a session.

The various types of meetings include regular meetings, special meetings, annual meetings, adjourned meetings, mass meetings, board of director's meetings, conventions, committee meetings, and executive sessions. Let us look at each one of these briefly.

- **Regular Meeting** — These meetings will be listed in your bylaws and are held anywhere from weekly to monthly to quarterly.

- **Special Meeting** — This is a meeting that is called for a particular reason, to be held at a designated time to take care of a matter at hand. When the meeting is called, then it must list the reason for the meeting and also the time and place. This information must also be provided to each member of the group. These meetings are by and large held for emergency purposes, and no other business is conducted at that time.

- **Annual Meeting** — This is the organization's yearly meeting and involves some of the bigger items that need to be addressed by all the members. For example, electing new officers will be a point of business at most annual meetings, and examining the yearly reports of the organization could be another agenda item.

- **Adjourned Meeting** — This is a meeting that is taking up where another meeting left off and can occur either on the same day or a different day. For example, if someone in the group suggests the meeting be continued for the completion of unfinished business then the new meeting would be an adjourned meeting. The meeting that was originally held and the meeting that is called the adjourned meeting are actually one meeting and considered as such.

- **Mass Meeting** — A meeting that is not "organized" but is made up of the group to discuss common goals for the organization.

- **Board of Directors Meeting** — This is a meeting of those who have been elected into the board positions and who are making decisions for the group. Normally, these meetings are not made up of more than just the board, and outside guests are not invited.

- **Convention** — This is when the entire group of delegates meets. These meetings frequently last more than one day, and representatives come together to make decisions for the group. A good example is the Democratic National Convention.

- **Committee Meeting** — This is a meeting of a group from the larger group who have been appointed or elected to take care of a certain item of business. It deals only with the one topic it has been assigned.

- **Executive Session** — These meetings are held in secret and/or are not open to the public. Minutes of the meeting are not disbursed to the general public, and members who are there are held to confidentiality. Often, city council might adjourn into executive sessions to discuss points that were not discussed at the open meeting such as the hiring and firing of a City Manager, for example.

CASE STUDY: TOM TORLAKSON

Tom Torlakson

Senator representing California's Senate District 7, which includes most of Contra Costa County

Senator Tom Torlakson

P.O. Box 21636

Concord, CA 94521

www.tomtorlakson.com

Born in San Francisco, California, in 1949, Tom Torlakson served in the Merchant Marine during the Vietnam War and earned a bachelor's degree in history in 1971, a life secondary teaching credential and an master's degree in education in 1977 from UC-Berkeley. Like many senators and government officials, Torlakson uses Robert's Rules of Order on a daily basis during the many meetings he attends. Recently appointed to chair the Senate Appropriations Committee while also serving as a member of the Education Committee and the Transportation and Housing Committee, Torlakson has more than his fair share of time adhering and leading groups in the appropriate Robert's Rules protocol.

Torlakson is also the chair of the Senate Select Committee on Schools and Community and noted, "I would encourage anyone who either participates in or oversees government meetings to simply read up on Robert's Rules of Order the same way they would read through a state's public meetings law, open records law, or any other background material relevant to your role. You do not need to be an expert by any degree — just get familiar with the basics so you know where to look when questions arise."

Of the 20 bills Torlakson sent to Governor Arnold Schwarzenegger in 2006, 18 were signed into law, including legislation to streamline and improve California's after-school programs and provide $2.9 billion in additional funding to the state's lowest-performing schools.

"As chairman of the California State Senate Appropriations Committee, I use Robert's Rules of Order to conduct hearings and maintain an orderly process. The rules are generally well understood by my fellow senators, many of whom had prior local government experience before being elected to the state legislature."

CASE STUDY: TOM TORLAKSON

Torlakson has also previously served as chair of the Senate's Majority Caucus, chair of the Senate Transportation and Housing Committee, and on the Senate Local Government Committee. An avid triathlete, Torlakson uses this knowledge as the chair and founder of the California Task Force on Youth and Workplace Wellness, a group seeking to raise the profile of health and fitness in the public schools and in the workplace.

His career in public service began as a science teacher in 1972. He was elected to the Antioch City Council in 1978 and then served on the Contra Costa Board of Supervisors for 16 years. The rest is history, as his Robert's Rules of Order training began during this time. He was elected to the California's 11th Assembly District in 1996 and 1998, followed by his election to the State Senate in 2000. He was reelected without opposition in 2004.

"I learned [Robert's Rules of Order] as a City Council member in Antioch, California, and later as a County Supervisor in Contra Costa County, where I served 16 years in office," he said. "This experience helped me use and understand the rules on a regular basis for many years during both board of supervisors meetings and committee meetings, as well as on other local boards and commissions."

Although used for only regular legislative hearings in his current positions, Torlakson said that Robert's Rules have helped him throughout his career in politics because the rules help maintain an orderly process, particularly when elected officials disagree on a policy issue and need a framework to guide discussions, make motions, and conduct votes. "The rules provide a baseline process that everyone needs to honor regardless of their opinions."

Although Robert's Rules of Order do make meetings run smoothly, Torlakson also noted that there are times when the rules are hard to follow. For example, he said, when motions lead to questions, which most do as a rule. "[This is] particularly [true] when officials want to conduct discussions that go beyond the limitations of Robert's Rules of Order. I have used the Rules for many years, am generally familiar with the specifics, and can explain details to most people who have questions."

Torlakson mentioned that Robert's Rules do allow for meetings to run much smoother than they otherwise would because, he said, "In general, it helps to remind people that some motions are not debatable. This keeps meetings progressing in an orderly fashion."

CASE STUDY: TOM TORLAKSON

As far as groups trying to learn and apply Robert's Rules, he said that it is true that groups do have a hard time learning to follow all the details in the rules. After all, the rules are quite extensive and overwhelming at first glance.

"But the Rules make sense and are more easily understood as groups get more familiar with the process," he added.

As for what is the hardest ruling that most chairs have to make when applying Robert's Rules he said that, for the most part, it seems to be closing debate. In its own way this poses a set of challenges, because most people want to keep talking and express their opinions even when the time has come to take a vote.

"Everyone needs to understand that any government meeting needs to proceed in an orderly fashion," Torlakson added.

At local meetings when folks are not familiar with Robert's Rules, a city councilperson is the best person to explain the rules to those who have questions Torlakson said. This can especially apply when members of the public are in the meeting and are not sure how the rules work.

As for moving into the information age and laying the groundwork for the successful use of Robert's Rules of Order electronically, much can be done to improve current conditions.

For example, Torlakson said, "It always helps to think before you write something down, especially when writing an e-mail. Generally, the best rule for elected officials is to think about any e-mail as if it were to be printed in the local newspaper. That helps people understand the consequences of getting beyond the intended audience."

Indeed, moving into the electronic age with Robert's Rules of Order might not be easy, but it can be easier when a person thinks before he writes.

Chapter 3

Election of Officers

All deliberative assemblies need leadership who is capable of conducting business that is on topic and efficient. Robert's Rules define several different offices that are important in the functioning of any group. In any group, the leaders will make or break the entire unit; therefore, thinking carefully about elected officials is a task that every member of the group must take seriously. Likewise, when a person takes on a role of leadership in a group, he or she should immediately become familiar with the bylaws and rules of that particular governing body.

This will depend on the size of the board members or executive board, among others. This number is also pointed out in the bylaws and should be adhered to as closely as possible.

Role of the Presiding Officer

The presiding officer or president of an assembly, more often than not called the chairman, is in the position to lead the assembly or group. Specific duties of this position should be defined in the bylaws of the organization. The term "chair" is used to refer to the person who is presiding over the meeting, even if it is not the presiding officer of the assembly. This is because of the person's physical position in the hall where the meeting is held. Robert's Rules recommend a chair in a raised and prominent location that is separate from where people will rise to make reports or address the assembly.

The importance of the role of the presiding officer in leading the assembly highlights how serious a matter it is when choosing someone for the position. The person should be selected carefully for his or her supervisory abilities. He or she should also be familiar with parliamentary law, the bylaws, rules of the organization, and goals of the assembly or group as a whole. It is also important that the person chosen for this position be tactful and able to navigate complicated social situations with ease. Inevitably, there will be situations when there are no rules to go by or bylaws that address the issues on the table. For this reason, it is equally important that the person chosen for the position of presiding officer have a strong dose of common sense, as the final ruling on many issues will come down to him or her.

Presiding officers are required to lead the assembly in specific legislative ways and also certain symbolic ways. Robert's Rules give the following suggestions to persons who are chairs of assemblies. Making sure to maintain a businesslike, formal atmosphere and avoid personal slander is always one of the key roles of the presiding officer.

1   Speak of yourself in the third person to reiterate that the decisions and statements made by the chair are not made based on personal bias.

2. In the same way, all persons addressing the chair

should use the term "The Chair" or "Mr./Madam Chairman."

3. In the same way, the chair should refer to members as "members" whenever possible to maintain the focus on the business at hand and not personal relationships.

Too often, assemblies overlook common-sense rules and get bogged down in bickering among individuals where rulings by the chair are taken personally, sometimes even made personally. If this has become a tendency of your organization, consider returning to these formalities to help regain a focus on business proceedings.

Before undertaking to lead any assembly, it is important that the presiding officer be familiar with and comfortable with the duties of a presiding officer. Robert's Rules outline 11 duties of a presiding officer:

1. Open the meeting.

2. Announce the order of the day.

3. Recognize members seeking the floor.

4. Bring a motion to close by restating, calling for the vote, and announcing the results of that vote.

5. To maintain the focus of the meeting, refuse to recognize frivolous motions.

6. Enforce the rules during a debate.

7. Expedite business.

8   Decide if a question is out of order.

9. Respond to a member requesting information, parliamentary or otherwise, that pertains to business.

10. Sign all business done by the assembly where necessary for purposes of authentication.

11. Conclude a meeting with proper adjournment.

To perform the duties, especially providing information as necessary (#9) to members of the assembly, it is vital that the presiding officer have the following documents present and on hand at each and every meeting:

1. Bylaws or other rules of the organization.

2. Parliamentary authority (Robert's Rules) and necessary subsequent parliamentary procedure information: this book or whatever is required to help you understand your parliamentary authority.

3. A list of all committees and their members.

4. A written agenda. It is helpful, but not essential, to bring copies of this for everyone in attendance — see the next chapter.

Other common-sense rules that presiding officers can follow include:

1. Starting the meeting on time, which makes everyone happy. Be sure there is a quorum present though; if not, you cannot take care of any legal business.

2. Stay organized and on track. Keep to the agenda, and do not let other members stray off point.

3. Come ready for questions and comments that might be directed toward you about agenda items. Also, try to get a sense of how many voting members are for or against the items on the agenda. The bottom line is following the bylaws.

4 Explain procedure when there is a question, and be sure to treat everyone with respect regarding his or her questions or any confusion there might be pertaining to an issue on the table.

5. Be fair and give everyone a chance to speak and say his or her side.

6. Do not lose control of the meeting. Members should speak only when you have recognized them to do so. If other members interrupt or disrupt the meeting, it is your job to put a stop to it. Sometimes, it is necessary to call a short recess to get the meeting back on track. Also, members should not be holding conversations among themselves while another member has the floor.

7. No matter what happens, stay calm, cool, and collected.

The Role of the Vice President

The vice president of the group or organization will take a key role in handling meetings in the absence of the president. In city councils, the vice president is called a mayor pro tem, which means he or she temporarily handles the meeting in the mayor's absence. If there is one vice president, then everything is forthright when the president is absent; conversely, some organizations have more than one elected vice president, which can begin to complicate matters. There is another position called president-elect, but again, it depends on the bylaws as to who will take the position of president in that person's absence. It is not always the president-elect who does this.

In any event, the person who it states in the bylaws takes over the meeting in the event of the president or presiding officer's absence should first and foremost be familiar with the duty of the president. This includes how to run meetings, the ins and outs of the bylaws, and the workings of the group as a whole.

It is also important to note that when the vice president does take over the meeting in the president's absence, he or she is still not able to handle all the functions of the president. It will be stated in the bylaws what can and cannot be done in the president's absence. One example is the appointing of committees. If the bylaws say it can be done only by the president, then that will have to wait until the next meeting.

The Role of the Secretary

In addition to the role of the presiding officer, the only officer mandated by Robert's Rules is that of the secretary. The role of the secretary or clerk is that of the recording officer of the assembly. The secretary is in charge of keeping all the minutes, files, membership, and order of business for the assembly. The duties of the secretary, as outlined by Robert's Rules, are as follows:

1. Record the minutes.

2. Keep files of all committee reports.

3. Keep the membership roll.

4. Make the minutes available to all members.

5 Notify persons of their elections to offices and provide them with necessary documents to conduct their duties.

6 Provide credentials to delegates elected to attend conventions.

7. Sign all copies of acts of the society.

8. Maintain a record book.

9. Send written notification of upcoming meetings to all members and conduct all written correspondence on behalf of the society.

10. Prepare an agenda for the use of the presiding officer (exact specifications in Chapter 4).

11. In the absence of the president and vice president, call the meeting to order and preside in the election of a chair pro tem.

The secretary should be familiar with all these duties and create appropriate record-keeping strategies to maintain the records that are required. In Chapter 6, you will find a wealth of helpful advice about what is required in each of these records and how to keep them easily.

The minutes recorded by the secretary are legal documents and should be treated as such. A handy guide to remember what does and does not need to be recorded follows:

- Record every motion that was adopted and all motions that were not adopted.

- Record the name of the member of the group who made the motion to adopt.

- Record all reports by members of the group along with the specific name of each person who reported.

- Record information if anyone was named or elected to a committee or chair position.

- Keep a written record of the vote tally and who voted "yea" or "nay."

It is not necessary to record all information, and here are some items that do not need to be recorded from the meeting:

- What a certain member believes to be true or offers as a personal opinion

- Motions that a member of the group withdrew

- The name of the group member who seconded the motion

- Long reports that outline every word

Secretaries should type up the minutes to the meeting as soon as possible after the meeting is held. This helps to keep the memory fresh regarding items that might be forgotten if too much time elapses. Secretaries need to send the minutes to the presiding officer to review before posting or sending out to other members of the group.

Secretaries also attend the executive sessions and report those minutes and the motions made. When corrections are necessary on minutes, be sure and date them and be specific about the particular pieces of information that are being changed. You will also need to sign your name to the minutes and note the date of final approval.

The secretary is also responsible for keeping track of the members, who they are and the particulars of their membership status. The presiding officer will expect the secretary to have a copy of the bylaws at the meeting, the minutes book, committee member names and information, and ballots in case a ballot vote is needed; often, the secretary is also called on to read resolutions aloud at the meeting.

Role of the Treasurer

In an assembly that conducts any business with finances, it is necessary to have a third officer, the treasurer. This person is the financial secretary and maintains the logs of all monies held by the assembly collectively. It is always suggested that this position be held separately from that of the general secretary position for reasons of being able to cross-check each other's work and maintain a checks-and-balances system to avoid fraud. Also, the duties of a general secretary are already numerous, and adequate reporting and monitoring of finances grows with the size of the organization. By creating a separate position to handle this aspect of the organization, it is more likely to be adequately attended to as necessary.

The treasurer's responsibilities include maintaining written logs of the organization's finances, preparing a full annual report (or more frequent if required by the bylaws), handling the money of the organization, and preparing tax-related documents. It is also important to note that the specific duties of the treasurer will differ from organization to organization, depending on the amount of money handled by the organization and the purpose for collecting/earning monies. Specific duties of the treasurer could include:

1. Collect dues from members.

2. Record all monies receive/expended.

3. Write checks and distribute monies.

4. Sign checks (could also be done by the president).

5. Invest the organization's cash on hand to create positive growth.

6. Provide members with written statements of dues or earnings.

7. Account to membership body for the expenditures made during the year in an annual report.

In some cases with organizations that include large quantities of money or with a large number of members from whom to collect dues, the role of a financial secretary is created in addition to the role of the treasurer. In these cases, the role of the financial secretary as different from the treasurer should be clearly delineated in the job descriptions as they appear in the bylaws.

In most organizations, the treasurer will give a short recount of the monies at each regular meeting. If something is not right or a problem is foreseen, the treasurer will bring this to the attention of the assembly or group at that time.

Treasurers might also be in charge of creating the group's budget with an idea of what is going in and coming out throughout the fiscal year.

Other Officers

There sometimes arises a need for an officer to fulfill another specific function of an organization that requires the creation of another type of office. Robert's Rules outline the following additional offices that are common to organizations. To create elections for any of these positions, the position must be included in the bylaws of the organization or added as an amendment to the bylaws per the amendment process.

- **Directors** — Members of an executive board in addition to other officers. Their roles and duties should be delineated in the bylaws.

- **Historian** — Prepares a narrative account of the society's activities that will become a part of the official history on acceptance by the assembly.

- **Librarian** — If the society has a collection of written material, this person maintains and organizes the collection.

- **Curator** — Custodian of any objects of value that belong to the society.

- **Chaplain** — Leads religious devotions, invocations, and other services as requested by the assembly.

- **Sergeant-at-arms** — Also called a warden or warrant officer, this person is in charge of preserving order in the meeting hall and may also be in charge of setting up the meeting hall.

- **Doorkeeper** — Also called a guard, this person checks the credentials of persons entering the hall for a restricted meeting.

Although it is recommended that all these positions be elected, it is noted in Robert's Rules that only directors absolutely must be elected. If the bylaws allow, the other positions can be appointed instead of being elected, which brings up the next question of how to elect officers.

Soliciting Nominations

Strictly speaking, nominations are not required for an election to take place; in most practical situations, they are necessary. A nomination is a basic form of a motion that moves "that _____ be elected _____" which fills in the blanks with a nominee's name and desired position. If no method of nomination is prescribed in the bylaws or constitution of the assembly, then anyone can make a motion regarding the method that should be used. Nominations can come from the chair, the floor, a ballot, a mailing, or by petition. Here is a brief description of how to conduct nominations for each method:

- **Nominations from the Chair** — The chair can nominate persons for any committee or position except the nominating committee.

- **Nominations from the Floor** — A member needs not be recognized by the chair to make a nomination, nor is any second required. Members simply rise and say the nomination during the time initiated by the chair. The same person may be nominated for several different positions at once, but one person may not nominate multiple people for the same position. Nominations continue under the direction of the chair until all members wishing to nominate have done so. The chair should repeat each nomination until all nominations are made. Nominations occur for one office at a time and follow the order that the offices are listed in the bylaws.

- **Nominations by a Committee** — Most commonly, nominations for officers of a society are created by a nominating committee. The committee should be chosen in advance and given the list of offices needing nominations for elections during the annual meeting.

Nominating committees should be elected and never appointed, unless specifically defined in the bylaws, by the chair or president. Neither should the president be a member of it unless appointed otherwise.

Frequently, a nominating committee will develop a slate that lists only one nominee for each position. It is not prohibited for the committee to present multiple persons for one position, but it should not be required. Also, members of the nominating committee should not be prohibited from becoming nominees, because this would make appointment to the committee a way to ensure that they would not become nominees.

Once the committee has developed a slate for presentation to the annual meeting, it is recommended that the committee members contact the nominees and obtain their acceptance of the nomination. At the annual meeting, they shall present it when asked by the presiding officer. After the presentation of the slate, a minority opinion from the committee can present alternative nominations as well, should there be a dissenting voice. Once the report is formally presented, the nominating committee is automatically discharged unless one of the nominees withdraws and the committee needs to meet again to revamp the slate. After the presentation of the slate, the chair must also call for further nominations from the floor and allow for those nominations to be added to the slate in addition to the nominees presented by the committee.

• **Nominations by Ballot** — This allows all members present to nominate candidates for every office via a written ballot and allows the assembly an indication of voting behavior. This functions in the same way (although never in the place of) an election ballot with the difference of everyone who receives a vote being nominated. The teller's report then does not say the number of votes received for each person, only the names voted for. In addition to never allowing the nominating ballot to become the election ballot, it is out of order to use a nominating ballot to limit voting to leading candidates.

- **Nominations by Mail** — This functions in the same way as nomination by ballot but is done by the secretary mailing every legal member a nominating ballot and instructions for completion and return.

- **Nomination by Petition** — Sometimes, the bylaws will say that a nominee needs a petition of a certain number of members to be placed on the slate. This can be done by mail if necessary and is a good method for use when working with an incredibly large population or membership, such as a governmental election.

Presentation of the Slate

Once the chair, through the nomination process, has acquired a slate of nominees, it is then the responsibility of the chair to formally present the slate of nominees to the assembly for the election. If there are no further nominations, the chair moves the assembly to the voting stage by calling for the vote. The vote can occur in one of several ways, which should be determined ahead of time either in the bylaws, or barring that, by a special motion to decide the method of voting.

Voting Procedures

There are several ways in which to conduct the actual election, many of which are similar to the methods of voting for a regular motion, which will be described in Chapter 5. The methods for voting in an election, as described by Robert's Rules are as follows:

Ballot Election

There are two basic ways of voting by ballot in an election. The first is the quickest and most efficient way of voting by ballot, in which the complete slate is determined before the ballots are distributed. The second, which offers more flexibility in choosing officers, calls for the balloting to happen immediately following the nominations for each office.

In either situation, if there is a tie or if none of the nominees secures the majority needed to be appointed to the position, there will be a need for subsequent ballots to be taken. If a repeat ballot for an office is necessary, all nominees remain on the ballot unless one or more withdraws his or her name. Although bylaws may create special rules that require a nominee to step down if one is not one of the front-runners in a runoff election, this is not required or suggested by Robert's Rules. Indeed, it may be the case that one of the nominees receiving fewer votes on initial ballots may win on subsequent ballots because he or she is seen as a compromise. Also, in both situations, if there is only one person nominated for an office, he or she still needs to be placed on a ballot and voted on if the bylaws call for a ballot election.

When electing a board or committee consisting of multiple vacancies, voting happens in the following manner for an example board of four members with six nominations to fill the positions. On the ballot, all six are listed as nominees, and voters are invited to choose four that they would like to see on the board but can vote only once per nominee. For each person that votes for him or her, each nominee is considered to have one vote. When the votes are tabulated, those who receive a majority of the votes are elected. In the event that more than the open positions receive a majority vote, the ones with the top number of votes are elected. If fewer than the number of positions receives a majority vote, those who do have a majority are considered elected and the rest of the nominees remain on the ballot for a run-off. This also happens when persons are tied for the lowest number needed to be elected to a position — those persons remain on the ballot for the run-off election.

Viva Voce Election

A viva voce election is used mostly in mass meetings or when a candidate is running unopposed. This type of election can be done by voice, rising, or a show of hands. Nominees are voted on in order of their nomination. Once a nominee for a particular office achieves a majority vote, he or she is considered elected, and the election for that office is closed, with it being assumed that the remaining nominees have voted "no." If members wish to vote for someone nominated later in the slate, they need to vote no for the early nominees. This process gives a strong advantage to those who are nominated early and is therefore not a suitable method for electing officers of societies. If the election is uncontested and the bylaws do not require a ballot, the chair can take a voice vote or declare the nominee elected by unanimous assent. In cases where the bylaws require a vote by ballot for elections, whether contested or otherwise, the assembly cannot make a valid viva voce election.

Roll-Call Election

Although highly unusual, a roll-call method of conducting an election ensures that each member of a society declares his or her preference for an office. In the case of a roll-call election, the process is the same as a standard roll-call vote (described in Chapter 5), and each vote should be recorded by the secretary.

Cumulative Voting

When electing positions held by more than one individual, whether by roll call or by ballot, a method called "cumulative voting" may be used. Much like the ballot method described earlier, this differs in that if there are four open positions on a board, each voter is given up to four votes for that board. Each may cast one, two, three, or four votes and may cast multiple votes for one person if one wishes. Although this method overrides the fundamental principle of parliamentary law of the right of the majority, this method of voting allows for a minority to achieve a voice on a specific delegation or committee by pooling all their votes for one person.

Transition Procedures & Etiquette

According to Robert's Rules, an election is final if the

nominee is present and does not immediately decline. In this case, the elected official's position will commence immediately. Frequently, this is impractical in action. The bylaws may say otherwise, that the elected official's position will more often than not be defined by a term, which will start at a later date. It is by and large a good idea to define terms in your bylaws, as this practice gives newly elected officials time to gain a deeper understanding of their expected role, prepare for transition, and properly say goodbye to the previous person who has served in that role. Many persons are unprepared to take over a new leadership role during an assembly that they came to as a general member.

For the position of presiding officer and secretary, it is especially important to create a smooth transition between one officer and the next. Some societies solve this problem by electing a president-elect a few months to a year before the term of the current president ends so that the transition is made smooth by the time given for the newly elected official to understudy with the current president by watching how he or she conducts business and manages the affairs of the society. It is vital to note that this practice can have problems associated with it. In cases where there is a strong division within the society and the president and president elect are from different factions, it may undermine the activities of the current president to have a president-elect in office. For this reason, the time given to any overlapping of offices should be carefully thought out before their inclusion into the bylaws.

CASE STUDY: CORY SPILLMAN

Cory Spillman

Cedar Hill, Texas, City Council Mayor Pro Tem & Oil and Gas
Marketing Representative for Hunt Oil Company

http://ci.cedarhill.tx.us/

Cedar Hill City Council Mayor Pro Tem Cory Spillman says that he uses Robert's Rules of Order at all the City Council meetings and board/commission meetings that he attends, as these rules have formally been adopted by the Council he sits on as the official parliamentary authority with some approved adaptations.

Spillman learned parliamentary procedure "on the job." He said, "I participated in meetings that utilized Robert's Rules of Order — trial by fire. I have since taken several courses," he noted.

He said he believes that Robert's Rules are helpful to any meeting. "I believe Robert's Rules of Order definitely assist in creating order in formal deliberative meetings. Robert's Rules of Order are especially important for meetings that involve large numbers of folks or deal with complicated discussions."

He has also experienced convention meetings where people used their knowledge of the rules to stymie debate and delay discussion and action on the real topics. He noted as well that with a strong chair or parliamentarian, these tactics can be put to an end quickly.

In addition to sitting on the city council of Cedar Hill, Texas, where he uses the rules, Spillman also noted that he has used Robert's Rules for church meetings, college society meetings, city board meetings, and conventions, to name a few. He does not however, recall a time when he used Robert's Rules for a for-profit business.

He noted one of the hardest rules to remember for people who are part of a meeting, leading a meeting, or even acting as a parliamentarian for a meeting. "I have never served as an official parliamentarian, but whether a person is chairing a committee or not, I believe the hardest rule to remember is order of precedence of motions.

"I believe it is difficult for groups to learn Robert's Rules of Order unless they actually use them consistently. Groups must make a commitment to follow the rules and stick to them. I have seen new homeowners' associations struggling to organize with

CASE STUDY: CORY SPILLMAN

no adopted parliamentary rules. Those organizations that make the early effort are rewarded by more efficient and orderly meetings for the long term."

For presiding officers who have to make rulings, Spillman said he believes the hardest ruling to make is keeping the debate balanced.

"Keeping the debate balanced requires that the chair order the speakers," he said. "I have experienced situations where board members feel cut off or put off if they are put near the end of the speaking list. Additionally, enforcing speaking time limits sometimes requires the chair to cut off individuals."

Spillman's favorite rule is "motion to adjourn," he said jokingly. "Actually, I like the rule to move the previous question. If debate becomes circular or repetitive, then a member of the council can use this motion to end debate on the pending motion."

There have been times at meetings when Robert's Rules have made meeting experiences for Spillman go much smoother than might have been the case otherwise. He gives an example of one such time noting that he was invited as a guest to a neighborhood homeowners' association meeting/picnic.

"It was an outdoor meeting with voting members and other guests participating at the picnic," he recalled. "When the meeting was called, there were lots of distractions and lots of interested people contributing to the discussion of a divisive issue. Using Robert's Rules allowed the chair to keep control of the meeting and allowed both sides of the debate to be heard."

Spillman added that he has countless stories of organizations that have not adopted parliamentary rules and cited the associated disorganized debates that result.

"Robert's Rules enables the chair to coordinate and maintain control of the meeting, and it helps all participating members and observers have common expectations for debating items."

Although Spillman said he has never had the chance to help an organization adopt Robert's Rules of Order, he has helped familiarize people at meetings who were not aware of parliamentary procedure, coaching them and not allowing them to circumvent the rules.

Although the city council that Spillman sits on does use Robert's Rules, he added that the group has also adapted the rules to meet the needs of that particular city.

CASE STUDY: CORY SPILLMAN

"I have not used other parliamentary rules," he said. "However, our city has adopted Robert's Rules, but we made adaptations to fit our needs. We recently updated the requirements for putting items on the agenda and made our motions more flexible."

In an electronic age, Robert's Rules are being used more online and for teleconferenced meetings. Spillman said he does participate in many online and teleconference meetings, but he has not used the Rules or been asked to do so in a meeting.

As for any electronic meetings or mailing including e-mails, it is always a good idea to think about what is being written. Spillman concurred. "I would think that anyone who e-mails has encountered a situation where their words are misinterpreted. Before sending important e-mails I reread the content to verify that it conveys the intended message. I may even wait a period of time before reviewing the content to allow for a fresh look. If appropriate, I may have a second reader review the message for their interpretation. In general I try to use concise wording and common language while avoiding slang terms."

He also offered another good piece of advice, "If the material is particularly difficult, then I would utilize the telephone or face-to-face contact with follow-up documentation of the meeting minutes."

Though Spillman did not have any one story that might help someone learn about Robert's Rules and more thoroughly understand the principles of parliamentary law, he did note, "I cannot emphasis enough that you have to apply the rules to get benefit from the rules. Once you have a general understanding, then I think that taking a class can enrich your understanding. Attending meetings to observe and speaking with a parliamentarian can also strengthen your understanding."

~Chapter 4
Basic Meeting Format

It is important to have a format and outline to all meetings so that members know when items of business will arise, what to expect next, and when to present motions or pieces of business so that they will not be out of order. Most deliberative assemblies have a traditional structure to their meetings that may be enumerated in their bylaws. For those without, Robert's Rules define a basic structure that should be followed to create a smooth and timely flow of events.

Preparing an Agenda

Part of the job of the presiding officer is to make sure that the events of a meeting flow smoothly from one thing to another. This is done by preparing ahead of time an agenda for the meeting and then guiding the assembly so that it adheres to the structure set out for it. Many assemblies benefit from written agendas presented to all members before the commencement of the meeting or by displaying the agenda where all can read and follow along. All agendas should include the following:

1. The order in which events of the meeting will occur

2. Times (the time for opening, how long each section of the meeting is scheduled to take, time of adjournment)

3. Items known ahead of time that will be dealt with during the meeting

In addition, it is often helpful to provide members with copies of any motions pending that are known of ahead of time.

The secretary needs to work with the president and other board members to put the agenda together for the meeting. The agenda will list all the items that need to be voted on or discussed by the members. Committees and officers more often than not get time on the agenda to go over their business, and the bylaws will note the order this should be done. There is no need to list officers or members who do not have a report to give, as this takes up time that can be used elsewhere. Also, make sure to add business from any earlier meetings that was not finished.

Certain meetings throughout the year might require certain business to be conducted. A good example of this is when new city officials are elected and must be sworn into office at the first meeting they attend in their new position.

Appendix 1 offers examples of meeting agendas, minutes, notices, and special meeting minutes as examples.

Achieving Quorum

Quorum is one of the simplest and most fundamental

of Robert's Rules, but it is also one that is frequently misunderstood and not followed. The idea of quorum is to protect against action in the name of the deliberative assembly without representation or approval by that assembly. Quorum refers to the number of voting members that must be present so that the society's business can be legally conducted. Like many of the specifics in Robert's Rules, the definition of quorum should be placed in your organization's bylaws. In the absence of a numerical or percentage definition in the bylaws, quorum is defined in these ways by Robert's Rules:

1. **For Mass Meetings** — Whoever shows up.

2. **Groups Without Enrolled Membership** — (For example, churches) whoever shows up.

3. **Conventions** — Most of those delegates registered to attend.

4. **Any Other Assembly** — In any other type of assembly where there is a defined membership, quorum is understood to be a majority of all the members.

There is no set number of members that will be suitable for all societies, which is why the definition of quorum in a society's bylaws is so important. Robert's Rules recommend that for organizations that rely on voluntary membership that the number required for quorum be set far below the majority. Although this may seem pessimistic, it is a practical suggestion due to the increasing amount of pressure placed on a volunteer's time these days. To determine quorum of a committee, either use a majority of all committee members or the definition of quorum set in the bylaws or by the parent organization. It is significant to note that a committee does not have the power to set its own quorum.

If you need to change the quorum definition in your bylaws, make sure to do so with care, as once the provision is removed, quorum immediately becomes the majority of all members. This could have disastrous ramifications because there may not be a quorum of this size present, and any further actions by the body could be technically voided. Therefore, the best procedure is to strike the provision and insert a new one all in one question.

If no quorum is obtained, you cannot conduct business. All that can be done by those present is to adjourn, recess, or take steps to achieve quorum. When the bylaws say that a meeting must be called at a certain time and quorum is not achieved, it should be noted that this requirement is still fulfilled, even though no business has been conducted. To achieve a quorum, there is a motion called a "Call of the House," which can be used in assemblies that have legal power to compel attendance of members. In the following use of this motion, unexcused members can be brought to the meeting under arrest. For this reason, it cannot be used in voluntary societies.

There might be other situations in which a quorum is needed and you need to hold the meeting at the time in which you have gathered. Some ideas for achieving quorum might be as easy as recessing and calling the members who are absent, allowing them time to arrive to the meeting place.

If there is an emergency that must be addressed and a quorum is not present, then you have to take matters into your own hands. Keep in mind, even if everyone in attendance votes in the same way, without a quorum it is still no good. The truth is you can still take an action in the name of the organization if you must, but the members of the group can call you to task for making the decision if they do not agree with it. In that case there might be a motion to ratify the action you have taken, and that would reverse the decision you made at the meeting missing the quorum.

Call to Order

Once it is determined that quorum has been achieved, the presiding officer takes his or her seat. Signaling for quiet, whether by a gavel or other sign, the presiding officer then says, "This meeting will come to order." Many times, this call to order is followed by a religious ceremony or patriotic exercises. More than just being a tradition, following a call to order with a specific group exercise or ceremony can have a unifying effect on the group.

Business

The bulk of a meeting is taken up by what is referred to as business. This includes the following:

Reading and Approval of Minutes

In most societies, the secretary reads the minutes from the previous meeting at the start of the meeting. The chair says, "The secretary will now read the minutes," and the secretary proceeds. This should immediately follow the outlining of the day's agenda by the presiding officer. If the minutes have been transcribed and mailed to each member before the meeting, the verbal reading of the minutes may be skipped unless there is an objection. After the minutes are read, the chair says, "Are there any corrections to the minutes?" If there are proposed corrections to the minutes, these are frequently dealt with on the basis of unanimous consent. Once all corrections have been made, the chair says, "If there are no [further] corrections to the minutes, they stand approved [as read or as corrected]." The secretary then records the corrections in the text of the minutes of the meeting corrected and simply notes in the current meeting's minutes that the minutes were corrected and approved. Make sure that if copies of the minutes have been provided to board members, council members, the city manager, etc., that only the secretary's corrected copy (or retyped copy) is used as the official record.

Reports from Officers, Boards, and Committees

Reports from all standing and special committees, boards and officers, although necessary at annual meetings, are not regularly required at regular meetings. The best practice is for the chairperson to call for a report only from a specific person or committee who is known to have a report to make by saying, "May we have the treasurer's report?" This avoids the tendency for committee chairs and officers to come up with something to say or reread the minutes of their last meeting when there is nothing that needs come to the attention of the assembly. If the chairperson is unsure as to whether a report is necessary, he or she may ask, "Is there a report from the program committee?"

In the event that an officer brings something to the attention of the assembly that requires action, he or she cannot make a motion toward that action himself or herself. Instead, he or she must complete his or her report and another member must move on his or her recommendation. This is opposite of a committee's report, where the committee member making the report can immediately make any necessary motion to bring the action before the assembly for consideration. If one of these motions occurs, it takes precedence over the rest of the meeting and is taken up immediately. If there was a motion on the table pertaining to one of these reports, it can be taken up at this time.

Officers, boards, and standing committees proceed in the order in which they are listed in the bylaws. In the case of special committees, they are required to report only when they are prepared and have been instructed to report. When a special committee's report is presented, any related motions on the table can be taken up at that time.

Reports of Special Committees

As previously stated, the reports of special committees come after the reports of the officers, boards, and standing committees.

Special Orders

A special order is an item of business that takes precedence over almost everything else. These are things that are brought before the assembly that need immediate action and attention. When a special order is created, it is assigned a specific time or date to be addressed. Because a special order overrules the rest of the business at hand, it requires a two-thirds vote to make an order of the day a special order. If the bylaws require a specific item to be considered at a specific meeting time/date (such as nominations), these may be considered under the heading of special orders without the necessary two-thirds vote.

Unfinished Business

Unfinished business refers to business that was on the table at the adjournment of the last meeting and that needs to be taken up again at the current meeting. It does not refer to old business, which has been completed and need not be revisited.) "Old business" is also an out-of-style term these days.) If a special meeting was scheduled to take up the tabled business, it should not be taken up during the next regular meeting; it should remain on the table until its scheduled time.

General Orders of the Day

General orders of the day refers to something that has been made an order of the day without becoming a special order. This sort of situation would happen when a question is either postponed or scheduled for the current meeting. It is important to note that the chair should never ask for unfinished business but should present the topics to be discussed as they were scheduled. If none were scheduled, this heading is skipped completely.

New Business

Once all pending business has been dispensed, the chair then opens the floor up to the members by asking, "Is there any new business?" The chair must ask this question and allow members with legitimate business to obtain the floor and make motions. The chair cannot rush through this heading or skip over it.

Announcements/Personal Privilege

After the business at hand has been conducted and before the closing of the meeting is a wonderful time for the chair to set aside a specific portion of the meeting for announcements and moments of personal privilege for the members of the assembly to share with each other. By setting this time apart and placing it on the agenda, the chair can limit the amount of this that goes on during the conduct of the business at hand. By placing this time at the end of the meeting, persons will tend to self-regulate their time in a desire to close. Also, this will ensure that this time does not detract from completing the business at hand.

Closing

At the end of the business and after the announcement time (if applicable), someone on the floor can "move to adjourn until _____." The chair can also call for this motion to be made. It should always be part of the motion that the time of the next meeting is stated so that the time is set with all the persons present to hear it. This will cut down on the need to contact and remind members constantly about the next meeting time.

Using Agendas

A note needs to be made here about the importance of using agendas. It speeds meetings up and keeps everyone on track during the time spent in discussions. Agendas should be easy to understand. Members of the leadership and those in attendance will be receiving the agenda, and everyone in the room needs to be able to use them effectively.

In the above paragraphs an outline of how meetings are called to order was addressed; however, there is also what is known as Robert's Rules Basic Agenda, and this is just as easy to use and takes the guesswork out of meeting planning and the actual meeting itself.

1. **Call to Order** — This is always necessary, even in the most basic of meetings. The chairman can rap on the podium with the gavel, and it is done. The meeting is open. It is also a good idea to start the meeting on time. Of course, if a quorum is not present, you might have to wait.

2. **Opening Ceremony** — This is a prayer or a patriotic action such as the Pledge of Allegiance.

3. **Roll Call** — This is often not necessary if is easy to see who is and who is not present, but if your bylaws call for this action, then it must be done as a matter of business for the meeting to be run correctly.

4. **The Consent Agenda Items** — These items are often voted on all at one time unless one of the officers pulls an item for individual discussion. You can expect that most of the items will be business that is not controversial and that the voting body will all agree on as a matter of course. The approval of past meeting minutes falls into this category.

5. **Regular Agenda Items** — These are items that are to be discussed and voted on individually. In legislative meetings such as city council meetings, public hearings might be held before this section, as the hearing results will be voted on during the regular agenda items section.

6. **Good of the Order** — This is the time when members can offer comments with no motions being made. This might also be a time when the public can make comments, as in city council meetings when the citizen comments are addressed.

7. **Announcements** — This is when members can make announcements pertaining to issues relating to the organization.

8. **Guest Speakers or Special Reports** — This is the time when reports are given by special committees or those approved by the group beforehand. This item can go anywhere here on the agenda and does not have to come as the last item.

9. **Adjourn** — this is the end of the meeting, and again, the chairman may hit the podium with his or her gavel and declare that the meeting has come to an end.

CASE STUDY: KARRI VALENZUELA

Karri Valenzuela

Executive Assistant

Formerly of Resolution Trust Corporation

Currently IMC2 — Executive Assistant to the President

Working as an executive assistant means that you know more than your boss — or as least as much as your boss. When Karri Valenzuela became an executive assistant at Resolution Trust Corporation, she had the chance to learn about Robert's Rules of Order on a first-hand basis while note-taking for her boss in executive meetings.

"I learned about parliamentary procedure through instructions from the chair," she said. Although not participating in the meetings herself, she said that indeed, she witnessed firsthand how Robert's Rules of Order do help make meetings run more smoothly.

"They [Robert's Rules of Order] allowed the meetings to be run in an orderly fashion. They ensured all topics were covered in a timely and respectful way," Valenzuela added.

The company where Valenzuela is currently employed also still uses Robert's Rules but in a revised way to meet the more informal needs of the corporate atmosphere, she said.

"My current company has moved to a more informal format," she noted. "We still utilize some aspects of Robert's Rules. For example, instead of 'tabling' a topic, we put it in the 'parking lot' for later discussion."

Valenzuela also noted that in her present job, meetings are held on a regular basis, which does not always work with Robert's Rules of Order.

"I find that the rules are a bit stilted in an organization where you meet regularly. Meeting on a daily or even weekly basis breeds familiarity and allows for a less formal meeting flow. That said, we do try to send an agenda of topics to be covered and the time required for each topic to make the meetings most efficient and productive. That is pulled directly from Robert's Rules."

Nevertheless, Valenzuela also says that anytime meetings have large numbers of participants — no matter how often that group meets — she believes Robert's Rules of

CASE STUDY: KARRI VALENZUELA

Order are necessary.

She said she has noticed that one of the hardest things for groups to learn when they begin to use Robert's Rules is that everyone must be given an opportunity to speak before a person who has already spoken can readdress an issue.

"It also seems to be hard for folks to remember to only make their comments to the chair. It is very easy to digress and begin speaking to individual debaters."

On that same note, Valenzuela explains that the hardest ruling that she has seen chairs have to make seems to be when to vote.

"Of course I also have my favorite rules," Valenzuela said. "That would be point of order because it is hard to always realize when rule infractions have occurred. Also, I like that only one person can speak at a time and must have the floor. It helps maintain order and civility, especially in heated debates, and sometimes that is really needed when folks get really worked up about an issue."

In the case of meetings that Valenzuela attended where a person was not familiar with parliamentary procedure, she said her company always included a short list of instructions on the back of the agendas.

With technology changing the way meetings are held these days, Valenzuela noted that she has found many things have changed and that electronic communication, such as e-mail, can certainly cause unnecessary misunderstanding at times.

"It is sometimes wisest to pick up the phone or schedule a meeting if there is a chance of misinterpretation of your comments. Just do it the old-fashioned way, and it works every time."

Chapter 5
Doing Business: Understanding Motions & Voting Procedures

Motions are the heart of the matter. Understanding motions and their correct usage is the foundation of Robert's Rules and is how business is conducted in deliberative assemblies. To make, discuss, amend, and vote for a motion is quite literally how a deliberative assembly does things. Unless you have a strong understanding of using and working with different types of motions, it is likely that you will not be able to get anything done as a member of a society.

What is a Motion?

A motion is the way in which someone introduces business to the floor. The types of motions include:

1. Main motions

2. Subsidiary motions

3. Privileged motions

4. Incidental motions

5. Motions that bring a question again before the assembly

To help you understand each of these classes of motions and their qualities, here is a brief description of each:

Main Motions

Main motions are the vehicles that bring business before an assembly. A new main motion can be introduced only when there are no other main motions currently being considered by the assembly. There are two distinct types of main motions, which are differentiated by their subject matter.

- **Original Main Motions** — These are motions that introduce completely new pieces of business to the assembly. These are the most often used types of motions and sound something like, "I move that the church hire a new pastor." Original main motions can be made verbally or in writing, depending on their complexity.

- **Incidental Main Motions** — These are main motions that grow up out of something else that happen in a meeting. For example, an incidental main motion might be a motion that arises from the reading of the day's reports.

Making Your Motions Correctly

When you make a motion, you need to do it correctly. For the most part, it is important that people in the meeting know what the purpose of the main motion is. It is a starting point for all other motions and actions to be taken.

You can put your motion in writing to organize yourself,

and you might sometimes even be asked to present it to the chairperson in this form.

To properly word the motion here are some tips:

1. Using the words "I move that..."

2. You do not need to say, "I make the motion to...."

Secondary Motions

When is the right time to use a secondary motion? Just about every main motion that is addressed will need some sort of discussion for backup. Whether the group or its members like the motion, hate the motion, or just want to tweak the motion, this is when a secondary motion will come in handy.

Because a fundamental principle of parliamentary law is handling only one piece of business at a time, when a main motion is pending on the floor, there are certain classes of secondary motions that can bring additional business before the assembly in ways that are considered in order. Secondary motions are divided into three categories: Subsidiary, privileged, and incidental motions, in that order.

- **Subsidiary Motions** — These are motions, such as amendments, that arise as the assembly deals with the pending main motion and help the assembly to deal with the question at hand. In short, this motion says that you want to do something else with the main motion.

- **Privileged Motions** — These are motions, such

as adjournment or recess, that need action by the assembly and are allowed to interrupt the business at hand to be considered. In short, this motion says "Let us do something even though there is already a pending motion on the table."

- **Incidental Motions** — These motions, such as point of order, arise from the business at hand and deal with points of procedure. In short, this says we need to do another thing to deal with what is already pending as an existing motion.

Motions That Bring a Question Again Before the Assembly

Because of their unique qualities, these are motions that do exactly what their class says: they bring a previously considered question before the assembly. These types of motions, like main motions, can be made only when there is no other business before an assembly.

How a Motion Works

A motion's life cycle follows a basic pattern of six steps. Although some motions have special rules governing their handling, some motions do not need to be seconded or debated. Understanding the basic life cycle of a motion will enable you to understand how an assembly deals with business.

1. **Step One** — A member makes the motion by saying, "I move that..." or, in the case of a resolution, "I move for the adoption of the following resolution: 'Resolved,

that...'" A member who gains the floor when there are no pending motions more often than not makes a motion immediately or with a word or two of introduction. Because the member who proposes a motion will be granted the right to speak first during the debate of the question, speechcs should not be made at the time of proposing the motion. Once a motion has been made, that member should return to his or her seat until given the floor again by the chair for debate.

2. **Step Two** — Another member seconds the motion by saying, "I second the motion" without obtaining the floor. It is recommended for large assemblies that the person seconding the motion stand and say their name as well so that the second may properly be recorded by the secretary. Seconding a motion is not considered a show of support for the motion, simply voicing the desire that the question contained therein be brought before the assembly. It is interesting to note that a second is not required, but rather it is for the chair's guidance as to whether to bring the question before the assembly. If the motion comes from a committee or if it is a routine motion, which the chair knows to have large approval from the assembly, there is no need to wait on a second.

3. **Step Three** — The chair states the question by saying "It is moved and seconded that..." and then repeating the motion. If the motion is written, the chair can have the secretary read the motion instead of reading it himself or herself. A motion should be read or stated by someone other than the member

making the motion, but if the person was clear in its presentation, the chair can press forward without re-reading the motion. In this case, the members are entitled, if they ask for it, to have the motion re-read. If a motion has been made and seconded but the chair finds it to be out of order, he or she says, "The chair finds that the motion is out of order."

Until the chair states the question, the person making the motion has the right to modify it. Others can suggest that the person making the motion make specific modifications. These types of changes should be limited to items that would not cause debate because, although the motion is still the property of its owner, no debate on modifications are in order. If a motion has been seconded and is later modified, the person seconding has the right to withdraw the second. If the modification comes from another member, though, that is considered to be an implicit second and no other second is needed. Also, before the chair states the question, the person making the motion has the right to withdraw the motion.

Once the chair states a motion, it becomes the property of the assembly, and the member who originally brought it to the assembly retains only the right to speak first during debate. That person may no longer modify (except by amendment like any other member) or withdraw the motion before a vote.

4. **Step Four** — The members debate the motion with the maker of the motion being invited by the chair first to obtain the floor and speak to the motion. Debating

a question will be discussed in depth later, but it follows these three basics: 1) all members have the right to speak twice, and no more, on each question each day. 2) When debating, a member may not rise to speak a second time while anyone who wishes to speak for a first time has the floor. Speeches must be confined to the time period outlined in the bylaws, or ten minutes, which is typical. 3) Debate remains open until all members who wish to speak have exhausted their right to do so. Debate may be closed early by the order of the assembly on a two-thirds vote.

5. **Step Five** — The chair puts the question to vote, once it seems that debate has ended, by first asking if the assembly "is ready for the question." If there are no other attempts to debate the motion, the chair then restates the motion before the assembly and calls for the vote. It should be clear to members that a vote is being taken and what the effects of an "aye" or "no" vote are afterward. Unless there is a specific type of voting required by the bylaws, a voice vote is used.

6. **Step Six** — The chair announces the result of the vote immediately, once the result of the vote has been determined. For voice votes, the chair's judgment is what determines the more numerous side. If there is uncertainty, either by the chair or by a member who doubts the chair's judgment on the issue, a rising or show of hands vote can be taken. Once the result of the vote is determined, the chair states the results of the vote, whether the motion carries, a statement of the effect of the vote, and announcement of the next order of business. This takes the form of "The ayes

have it, the motion is carried. The church will build a new spire to better be seen from the freeway. We will now move on to announcements of birthdays."

In the fourth edition of Robert's Rules, the motion process is explained as below.

ORDER OF PRECEDENCE OF MOTIONS

The ordinary motions rank as follows, the lowest in rank being at the bottom and the highest at the top of the list. When any one of them is immediately pending, the motions above it in the list are in order, and those below are out of order.

Fix the Time to which to Adjourn — can be:

- Frequently privileged

- Not always privileged: Privileged only when made while another question is pending and in an assembly that has made no provision for another meeting on the same or the next day.

- Can be amended

Adjourn

- Frequently privileged

- Not always privileged: Loses its privileged character and is a main motion if in any way qualified, or if its effect, if adopted, is to dissolve the assembly without any provision for its meeting again.

Take a Recess

- Frequently privileged

- Not always privileged: Privileged only when made while other business is pending.

- Can be amended

Raise a Question of Privilege.

- Frequently privileged

ORDER OF PRECEDENCE OF MOTIONS

Call for the Orders of the Day.

- Frequently privileged

Lay on the Table.

Previous Question.

- Require a two-thirds vote for their adoption; the others require only a majority.

Limit or Extend Limits of Debate.

- Requires a two-thirds vote for its adoption; the others require only a majority.

Postpone to a Certain Time

- Debatable

- Can be amended

Commit or Refer.

- Debatable

- Can be amended

Amend.

- Debatable

- Can be amended

Postpone Indefinitely.

- Debatable

A Main Motion.

- Debatable

- Can be amended

*Source: **Robert's Rules of Order Revised** by General Henry M. Robert, 1915 Fourth Edition, Public Domain.*

Taking Up Business in the Correct Order

When working with parliamentary procedure, business moves forward by following correct procedure. This is a bit tricky to understand, but Robert's Rules work on a concept of priority that places the most immediate items in the highest priority and order of voting. On the other hand, instead of thinking of this as a priority system, it is perhaps better to understand it as a hierarchy. The main motion is at the top of the hierarchy, as it sprouts motions and amendments. Like a ladder, you must start at the bottom and climb to the top - clear the bottom level before moving up and voting on the next level.

Main Motions

Main motions are motions that bring new, original business or propositions before the assembly. Whether original main motions or incidental main motions, there are eight characteristics that Robert's Rules identify that define a main motion:

1. Cannot be made when there is another question pending.

2. Cannot be applied to another motion.

3. Someone else on the floor? Then a main motion is out of order.

4. Must be seconded.

5. Is debatable.

6. Can be amended.

7. Requires (by and large) a majority vote.

8. Can be reconsidered as a motion.

Members make main motions by obtaining the floor when there are no other main motions pending. Main motions can be submitted either verbally or in writing. If a motion is submitted verbally, the form of "I move that..." is used. Persons making verbal motions should take a moment to think through the wording of a motion before making it to cut down on time being spent on modifying the motion before the chair states it.

If a motion is submitted in writing, it is called a resolution, and writers of resolutions must follow a specific format in their composition. (See Appendix IV for a sample resolution.) This format takes the following form:

> Whereas... [preamble that provides brief background information on the motion to follow] and
>
> Whereas [another clause of the preamble if necessary] be it...
>
> Resolved, that ... [action to be taken]
>
> Resolved, that ... [action to be taken]

Each clause of the preamble and the resolution should be separately set off so that it is clear to the assembly the different points that are being resolved. It is a tendency of persons writing resolutions for the first time to use the preamble to argue the case of the motion. This should be strictly avoided and the preamble used only for necessary background information. When a motion with a preamble is considered, the preamble is always amended last because the changes to the resolutions themselves may cause changes to the preamble.

In some cases, a motion does not need to be seconded. For the most part, all motions do need a second; otherwise the motion is not valid. The second of a motion is done in part so that if only one person is interested in a question, then the remainder of the meeting will not be a discussion about an item that no one else is in favor of discussing. If the presiding officer has a general idea that the members are in favor of a discussion on the motion, then a second is not always necessary, but formality should rule nevertheless, so that there is no confusion. If no one immediately makes a second on a motion, the presiding officer can also ask if anyone would like to second the motion.

The fourth edition of Robert's Rules of Order details the exceptions to motions that need to be seconded; this has not changed over the years.

***Exceptions.* The following do not require a second:**

- Question of privilege, to raise a

- Question of order

- Objection to the consideration of a question

- Call for orders of the day

- Call for division of the question (under certain circumstances)

- Call for division of the assembly (in voting)

- Call up motion to reconsider

- Filling blanks

- Nominations

- Leave to withdraw a motion

- Inquiries of any kind

Subsidiary Motions

Subsidiary motions (a series of motions that get rid of the main motion on the table) are those secondary motions (a motion that is made while the main motion in question is still open and is a term that can be used for subsidiary, privileged and incidental motions) that help the assembly in dealing with or deciding on the main motion currently before them. Subsidiary motions include:

Postpone Indefinitely

Postpone indefinitely is used when the assembly does not want to take a position on the main motion currently before the assembly. This motion takes precedence only over the main motion that it is applied to; any other business cannot be interrupted to discuss or vote on this motion. A second must be obtained to consider the motion to postpone indefinitely, and the assembly has the opportunity to debate the motion. Uniquely from any of the other subsidiary motions, debate on a motion to postpone indefinitely can involve the merits of the main motion pending. If the motion to postpone indefinitely is rejected, it cannot be reconsidered; however, a carrying motion to postpone indefinitely can be reconsidered.

Amend

Amend is used to modify the wording of a pending motion. Amend is perhaps the most frequently used subsidiary motion. The same process is used to amend bylaws or something else already adopted, but is not then a subsidiary motion. It is especially important to note that a motion to amend a pending motion must be in the same bearing or subject as the pending motion. Amending the main motion should never be used to change it in such a significant way as to undermine the original intention of the main motion.

Amendments can be amended. A pending primary amendment, before being voted on, can be amended with a secondary amendment. This can lead to confusion and requires careful supervision by the assembly's leadership team to ensure that the members are clear when voting happens that they are not approving the primary amendment to the main motion, but the rewording of that amendment by a secondary amendment. Although amendments can be amended, secondary amendments cannot then be amended, because it would be far too confusing.

Amendments can happen in one of three ways, by adding to, subtracting from, or combing both to modify the wording of a motion.

- Adding to or inserting words places one word to several paragraphs into the motion before the assembly. When making an amendment of this type, it is important to identify the exact location to insert in the original amendment. Once an amendment has been voted on and words have been added, they cannot be removed or changed except by a reconsideration of the vote on the amendment.

- Striking out removes a word or paragraphs from the pending motion. In a motion to strike out words, they must be specifically identified and consecutive. To retain certain words within the words to be struck out, an amendment to the amendment must be made; once words have been struck, they cannot be reinserted.

- There are two combinations of these types of amendment actions which, when used as a combination, are considered one amendment, and the different parts cannot be separated into two different questions.

Strike out and insert is used to apply to individual words that should be removed and replaced. This type of an amendment can be used to replace a specific word or to strike out a word and insert another one in a different place (so as to retain the meaning of the motion).

Substitute is used to replace whole paragraphs, and using the word "substitute" should be avoided when speaking of strike out and insert of words. Substitute can be used in a secondary amendment, thus substituting a substitute that cannot be amended.

When an amendment is made, it must be seconded and can be debated. Even after an amendment has been carried, its merits can be debated as part of the debate of the main motion.

Commit or Refer

Commit or refer is used when there is a main motion before the assembly that needs further research or consideration before the assembly can make an informed decision. This motion sends the pending main motion to a committee where it can be considered in depth before the committee returns to the assembly with a recommendation. Because it puts a temporary end to discussion and amendments of the main motion, this subsidiary motion takes precedence over the main motion and subsidiary motions that would change the main motion (postpone indefinitely, amend, divide the question, consideration by paragraph). Conversely, if a motion to postpone indefinitely, limit or extend debate, or lay on the table exists, the motion to commit yields. The motion to commit can refer a motion to a committee of the whole, a quasi-committee of the whole, or to an informal consideration.

Motions to commit should include the method of consideration that will be used and the committee it will go to if being referred to a standing committee. If being referred to a special committee, it should set the requirements for the committee's formation. For both standing and special committees, the motion to commit should include instructions for their responsibilities and powers in relation to the motion to be considered. Motions to commit that do not include these necessary details should not be ruled out of order, but rather the members should offer suggestions or formal amendments to complete the required details of the motion.

Once a motion to commit to a special committee has been adopted, the necessary next order of business is to select the committee members who will serve. Although it is not necessary to include the person who made the motion to commit on the special committee, if he or she has the interest and qualifications necessary, there is no reason that he or she cannot serve. The chair will more often than not appoint the special committee, unless specifically designated otherwise, and designate a chairman. The committee, once convened, is free to consider all amendments and modifications to the motion without regard to what had previously been considered.

Postpone Definitely

This motion is used to postpone debate and consideration of a pending motion until a specific hour, day, time, or event. This is used when it would be more convenient or appropriate to consider a pending motion at a later time. Main motions with their associated subsidiary motions are all postponed at once.

There are some specifics as to what extent items may be

postponed. If more than a quarter of a year will pass before the next regular meeting, the motion cannot be postponed that long. Instead, the motion can be postponed to later in the same meeting, or an adjourned meeting can be convened and the motion can be postponed to that time. If less than a quarter will pass before the next regular meeting, the motion can be postponed no longer than the next regular meeting. For example, if an organization holds a general meeting only once a year, an adjourned meeting must be provided for, because more than one quarter would pass before the next regular meeting. On the other hand, if a society meets monthly, the motion can be postponed up to one month at the next regular meeting but not beyond that.

Once a motion has been postponed, it becomes a general order of the day for the meeting for which it was postponed. Unless it was specifically created as a special order, it will then be taken up after unfinished business under the heading "Unfinished Business and General Orders" in the agenda. When the motion is taken up again, any pending motions, including amendments, motions to postpone indefinitely, and motions to commit, are in the same state that they were when the motion was last before the assembly. If the motion is postponed beyond the current session, all limits on debate from previous speakers are lost, and everyone reverts to having the same two opportunities to speak.

Limit or Extend Debate

An assembly can exercise control over debate on a question in one of two ways, by limiting or extending debate or by previous question. The first, limiting or extending debate, is used to provide specific limitations (or remove them) from those who are participating in the debate. A motion to limit debate does so by either reducing the number or length of speeches allowed each member, or by setting a specific hour or length of time after which debate will be ended and the question put to a vote. A motion to extend debate can do so by removing or altering the regular rules of length and number of speeches allowed each member. A motion to limit or extend debate cannot end debate immediately. This is done using the motion of previous question.

The motion to limit or extend debate is not debatable, though it can be amended. If a motion to limit or extend debate is amended, the amendment, like the original motion, is not debatable. Motions to limit or extend debate suspend the standing rules of the society, and for this reason motions to limit or extend debate require a two-thirds vote, not a simple majority.

Previous Question

Previous question is the subsidiary motion used to end debate and vote immediately on one or more pending questions. When an assembly wishes to end debate on a topic currently before it, any member may "move the previous question." This motion ends all debate on the question at hand, which should be specified by the member making the initial motion. Adoption of a motion of previous question also prevents any other subsidiary motions from being made, except the motion to lay on the table.

This motion requires a second but is not debatable and

cannot be amended. Because adoption of a motion of previous question suspends the standing rules regarding debate, a motion of previous question requires a two-thirds vote to carry. If the motion fails to carry, debate on the pending question continues as if the motion to previous question had never been made. In the event of a failure to carry, the motion can be proposed again. Any motions to previous question can also be reconsidered at any time before the vote is taken on the previous question motion.

When a motion to a previous question is made on a string of motions, those motions must be subsequent to each other. For example, if there is (1) a pending main motion, with (2) a pending amendment with (3) a pending motion to commit, and with (4) a pending motion to extend debate, a motion to previous question can apply to 3 and 4, but also not only to 3. In the case where a previous question motion is carried on pending questions 3 and 4, the voting then continues immediately without debate between the votes. Voting occurs for a pending question, which will be made void by the voting that will happen on pending question 4. Once a vote has been taken on a pending question, it proceeds to the next question.

If in the course of voting on the three motions pending on the previous question motion, the pending motion to commit the amendments to committee is passed, the motion to previous question is understood to be exhausted. This is because a vote on the pending amendment no longer needs to be taken at the current session, because the amendment has been sent to a committee. When the committee returns with its recommendations to the assembly, debate and subsequent motions from the committee's recommendations are allowed, as the motion to previous question no longer applies.

Lay on the Table

Lay on the table is the motion with the most priority. A motion to lie on the table is used to temporarily set aside the pending motions before the assembly to enable the assembly to address an urgent matter of business. When pending business is laid on the table, there is no such set time for returning to it, but the business can be picked up again at the will of the majority.

This is one of the most misused motions in all of Robert's Rules. Ordinary societies frequently use this motion to do the work of the motion to postpone indefinitely. This is an abuse of the motion to lay on the table and an abuse of the fundamental principles of parliamentary procedure, because it gives the majority the ability to halt debate on a motion immediately and without debate. This use overrides the rights of the minority, and individual members and chairpersons should carefully watch to make sure their societies do not use it for this purpose.

Although the motion to lay the pending business on the table is not debatable, it is proper and in order for the chair to ask the person making the motion for his or her reasoning in asking for this motion. By questioning the member making the motion, the speaker can therefore determine the intentions of the person seeking to table the motion and decide whether the motion is out of order (because it should be a motion to postpone indefinitely) or warranted.

Motions to lie on the table require only a simple majority vote to pass and cannot be debated. They also cannot be reconsidered because it is faster and simpler to just take the business up from the table again. Business on the table of a deliberative assembly can be moved to be taken up by any member at a regular meeting. It can be taken up at a special meeting only if proper notification was given to all members of the society that the business would be addressed at the special meeting. If there will be no regular meeting in the next quarter, the matter must be taken from the table by the end of the current meeting session, or it dies.

From the fourth edition of Robert's Rules of Order, the subsidiary motions are laid out below. "In the following list the subsidiary motions are arranged in the order of their precedence, the first one having the highest rank. When one of them is the immediately pending question, every motion above it is in order, and every one below it is out of order. They are as follows:"

SUBSIDIARY MOTIONS	
Lay on the Table	28
The Previous Question	29
Limit or Extend Limits of Debate	30
Postpone Definitely, or to a Certain Time	31
Commit or Refer, or Recommit	32
Amend	33
Postpone Indefinitely	34

Privileged Motions

Call for the Orders of the Day

A call for the orders of the day is an extremely simple motion that demands the assembly do business in the proper order. This simple motion is of utmost importance at large general meetings or conventions where most of the work is done off the floor in committees. If the chair is doing his or her job and announcing the order of business and following the set agenda, there should be no need to use this motion. Should the chair miss a piece of an agenda or if the time for a special report or piece of business comes without the chair's notice, a member may rise and use a call for the order of the day to get the assembly back on track.

Although a specific instance is the most common cause for the use of this motion, members may give only a general call for the orders of the day to be followed and cannot ask to give one piece of business priority over another. If the chair requests, the person making the motion may remind the chair of what is scheduled.

This privileged motion gives the power to call for the orders of the day to any individual member of a deliberative assembly. There is no need to have a second for this motion, and it is not debatable or amendable. On one member requesting the call, it must be enforced. If the assembly wishes to set aside the orders of the day, this must be done by a two-thirds vote because it overrides the standing rules.

Raise a Question of Privilege

This privileged motion is used to request that a main motion relating to the rights and privileges of members be brought up immediately because of its urgency while business is pending. This can be used when a question would change the voting rights or membership status of members in such a way that the pending business would be affected. Other types of privilege might be points of personal privilege or privileges of the whole. An example of this would be raising a question of personal privilege for a member to excuse himself or herself from the meeting because a motion at hand would affect his or her pay scale. Or perhaps a matter of privilege that would affect the assembly would be one that would request the lights be turned up or the doors closed, so as to provide for a better environment for hearing and deliberating on the motions at hand.

When a question of privilege is raised, it need not wait for the floor to be open, depending on the urgency. Also, it cannot be voted on, amended, debated, or applied to any other motion. It is the chair's decision once the question has been heard as to whether to admit the request, and once made, that decision cannot be reconsidered. If the chair approves, the person raising the question of privilege can make a subsequent main motion if applicable and have it undertaken immediately. If a subsequent motion is made, that motion can be debated and amended like any other main motion.

Recess

A recess, like in elementary school, is a short break in the business of the day. After a recess, all business is resumed exactly at the point at which it left off, as if there had been no interruption. If there is a motion pending, the privileged motion to recess proposes taking a break immediately. If there are no pending motions, the motion to recess is a main motion.

A motion to recess should include a time (or be amended to include a time) and requires a majority vote. It cannot be debated or presented while someone else has the floor, and it must be seconded. Following a recess, the chair returns the assembly to order and restates the business before the assembly.

Adjourn

The motion to adjourn, when there is no other pending business on the floor, is a main motion. The privileged motion to adjourn is allowable only when there is some other provision made for another meeting. The motion to adjourn, whether there is pending business or not, requires a majority vote. If it receives a majority vote, the meeting is closed immediately. The majority should never be forced to continue in deliberation longer than it desires, as that would be a violation of fundamental parliamentary law.

One of three things happens when a motion to adjourn is carried. 1) If an adjourned meeting has been scheduled, the business of the current meeting will be resumed at that time as if no interval had passed. 2) In cases where the society has regular meetings, such as weekly or monthly meetings, the incomplete business of the current meeting is resumed during the unfinished business section of the next meeting's regular schedule of business. 3) If there is an occasion where the majority votes to adjourn the meeting with unfinished business when there is no provision for another meeting within a quarter, or if any of the members will end their term at the close, all unfinished business falls to the ground. At the next meeting, it may be reintroduced as if it had never been brought up.

Although there is no debate allowed on a motion to adjourn, there are several pieces of parliamentary business that can occur while a motion to adjourn is pending. The chair should inform members of pending business that requires attention before adjournment, and important announcements should be made. Motions to reconsider previous votes or minutes can be made. Notice can be given where required for motions that will be made at the next scheduled session. A time can be set for an adjourned meeting if there is none already set. Although any and all these topics can be addressed earlier, sometimes this is impossible, and if necessary, they can be considered while the motion to adjourn is pending.

If the motion to adjourn does not pass, business is immediately resumed where it was previously. After some business has been conducted, a motion to adjourn can be made again.

Fix the Time to Which to Adjourn

Fix the time to which to adjourn motion is used to set another time in the future when the business of the current meeting will be resumed. The motion to fix the time to which to adjourn to does not have any bearing on the adjournment of the current meeting. If there is a prescheduled time to continue the business, the motion to fix the time to which to adjourn is not in order. When in order, this motion should include specifics of location, date, and time when the adjourned meeting will be held. This creates what is called an adjourned meeting, which is separate and different from a special meeting. Special meetings are called out of the normal calendar of the society and require that notice be given to all members. Adjourned meetings, because they are simply continuations of previous meetings on later days, do not require notice and are not considered separate meetings for the purpose of minute keeping.

Motions to fix the time to which to adjourn are not debatable, and they can only be amended to define or change the date time or place. Once made, these amendments are not debatable. Voting requires a simple majority vote, and the decision can later be reexamined, as is sometimes the case when the assembly gets more done than expected earlier on. This motion, because of its nature, frequently gives rise to the privileged motion to adjourn.

Incidental Motions

An incidental motion is a procedural motion and could be brought up due to a question that is pending in the meeting. The incidental motion takes precedence over anything else on the table and must be taken care of before any additional business is taken up. An incidental motion is required to yield to a privileged motion, but this particular type of motion is not debatable, with the exception of certain situations. It is also important to note that an incidental motion may not be amended unless it is specifically relating to the division of a question. Neither is it allowed for a subsidiary motion to be used here, with the exception of it being amended or a debatable appeal.

Indeed, this means that some of these motions can be debatable and some can be amended; it depends on the situation.

Another point to note is that when an incidental motion is taking precedence, it must be related to the question at hand, and it cannot be made if a subsidiary motion is pending. This is because any objection can be related only to the original motion. The table below from the fourth edition of Robert's Rules gives an example of items that might come up relating to incidental motions:

INCIDENTAL MOTIONS	
Questions of Order and Appeal	21
Suspension of the Rules	22
Objection to the Consideration of a Question	23
Division of a Question, and Consideration by Paragraph or Seriatim	24
Division of the Assembly, and Motions relating to Methods of Voting, or to Closing or to Reopening the Polls	25
Motions relating to Methods of Making, or to Closing or to Reopening Nominations	26
Requests growing out of Business Pending or that has just been pending; as, a Parliamentary Inquiry, a Request for Information, for Leave to Withdraw a Motion, to Read Papers, to be Excused from a Duty, or for any other Privilege	27

Point of Order

There might be times when a member of the group feels that a meeting is not being conducted as it should. In this case, the term "point of order" is used. Perhaps the presiding officer is not keeping the other members to the rules. When "point of order" is made, it allows for the entire group to take note that a breach in the rules has been made and recognized. Accordingly, the presiding officer then needs to defend a ruling that has been made before moving on to the next discussion.

Appeal

Appeal happens when two more members of the group believe that something unfair or inaccurate has taken place in the meeting regarding a ruling that was officially made by the presiding officer. This motion must be seconded, but if it is, the next step is a vote by the group for that ruling to be voted on. That said, the vote may be for or against the original ruling, and if against, then it reverses the motion that had been previously made. An appeal is also debatable but only within certain guidelines as noted in Robert's Rules. For example, in this case, a member can only speak one time on the issue. The presiding officer has the right to speak before the vote in defense of what was ruled and before the final vote is called.

Suspend the Rules

A motion to suspend the rules applies when a group decides to do something that is not allowable in the actual rules it is supposed to follow. Even when the group does suspend the rules, it is still not allowed to break the bylaws or constitution of the amendments that are in place. Robert's Rules clearly define the rules that cannot be suspended, the main part of this being the bylaws period. Fundamental parliamentary rules are also not suspendible, and in the case that a rule being suspended might be unfair to an absent member, then it is not allowed either. Rules that can be suspended include items related to business practices. When a group does deem it necessary to suspend the rules, it might make sense to take care of this by a general consent where everyone agrees, as opposed to a motion that has to be voted on by the group. To suspend the rules, it must have a second, it is not to be debated, it is not to be amended, and it cannot be made while another motion is pending. The most important item to note is there needs to be a two-thirds vote.

Objection to the Consideration of the Question

In the case of an objection to the consideration of a question, a member of the group raises this issue when he or she feels that a motion coming before the group could cause some sort of harm if voted on or discussed. Robert's Rules also note here that this objection does not require that a second be made, it is not debatable, nor can it be amended down the road. For this to pass, it requires a two-thirds vote, and an objection to the consideration of the question must be made before the debate on the motion begins.

Division

When a division takes place, it means that a member of the voting group can request that the presiding officer confirm an existing vote. He calls out "division" to make his point known. The presiding officer then has to do a new vote in front of everyone to confirm the accuracy of it. For a voice vote, the presiding officer asks for a show of hands to recount; when it was a rising vote that has caused the division, then the presiding officer calls for a counted rising vote.

Division of a Question/Assembly

A division of a question, would take place when the motion has more than one piece to it and needs the specific pieces voted on separately. The requirements to be noted regarding the division of a question include the fact that the motion should have the ability to stand alone, it requires a member to make a second, and that it must have a majority vote to proceed. You might also hear this referred to as a division of the assembly, with the exception that the division of assembly requires a standing recount vote only.

Consideration by Paragraph or Seriatim

Consideration by paragraph is when a motion is taken paragraph by paragraph, with amendments to the motion be made as the meeting goes on. At the end of the entire document discussion, then a vote is made concerning the motion as a whole.

Requests and Inquiries

Many motions will fall under the requests and inquiries umbrella. These include parliamentary inquiry, point of information, and withdrawal of a motion.

Parliamentary Inquiry

A parliamentary inquiry takes place when parliamentary help is needed. A member may call this motion to address confusing issues that arise.

Point of Information

A point of information is a motion that is called when a

member of the group needs more information than has been previously given.

Request Permission to Withdraw or Modify a Motion

A member of the group may withdraw a motion he or she has made if a discussion has been had and the person who made the motion realizes it was not a good one. A motion to be withdrawn does not require a second, and the motion that was withdrawn does not need to be listed in the minutes of the meeting.

Request for Any Other Privilege

This would also fall under a request and inquiry and is considered on a case-by-case basis.

Motions that are Not to be Amended

Restorative Motions, Those That Bring an Issue Back, and Other Types of Motions

In some situations, there are motions that cannot be amended. According to the fourth edition of Robert's Rules of Order, these are listed below.

MOTIONS THAT CANNOT BE AMENDED	
To Adjourn (except when it is qualified, or when made in an assembly with no provision for a future meeting)	17
Call for the Orders of the Day	20
Question of Order, and Appeal	21
To Object to Consideration of a Question	23
Call for a Division of the Assembly	25
To Grant Leave to Withdraw a Motion	27
To Grant Leave to Speak after Indecorum	21

MOTIONS THAT CANNOT BE AMENDED	
A Request of any Kind	27
To Take up a Question Out of its Proper Order	22
To Suspend the Rules	22
To Lay on the Table	28
To Take from the Table	35
To Reconsider	36
The Previous Question	29
To Postpone Indefinitely	34
To Amend an Amendment	33
To Fill a Blank	33
A Nomination	66

MOTIONS THAT OPEN THE MAIN QUESTION TO DEBATE	
Postpone Indefinitely	34
Reconsider a Debatable Question	36
Rescind	37
Ratify	39

Motions that are Not Debatable

In some cases, a motion might not be debatable. Members of the group are still allowed to ask questions and make suggestions, just not debate the issue at hand. That said, the presiding officer should allow for simple comments before taking a vote on an undebatable motion.

The following is a list of motions that are undebatable, from the fourth edition of Robert's Rules.

UNDEBATABLE MOTIONS	
Fix the Time to Which to Adjourn (when a privileged question)	16
Adjourn (when unqualified in an assembly that has provided for future meetings)	17

UNDEBATABLE MOTIONS	
Take a Recess (when privileged)	18
Call for the Orders of the Day and questions relating to priority of business	20
Appeal when made while an undebatable question is pending; when simply relating to indecorum, or transgression of the rules of speaking; or to priority of business	22
Suspension of the Rules	22
Objection to the Consideration of a Question	23
Incidental Motions, except an Appeal as shown above in this list under Appeal	13
Lay on the Table	28
Previous Question [29] and Motions to Close, Limit, or Extend the Limits of Debate	30
Amend an Undebatable Motion	33
Reconsider an Undebatable Motion	36

Restorative Motions

Restorative motions give the voting group a chance to change its mind on a motion if needed. The motion goes against the grain of typical parliamentary rules, which normally notes that when a motion has been determined, it cannot be changed at the meeting in which it was voted on either for or against. Of course, with exceptions to rules, Robert's does note that changes can be made, as invariably situations do arise when a motion needs to be recanted. There are two motions that are used often when restorative motions are called: rescind and reconsider.

Rescind

To rescind an item means to get rid of the motion that has been adopted. This can apply to bylaws, resolutions, or anything else that has been adopted by the voting group. That said, there are of course rules that apply as well. If an action has been taken on an amendment that was adopted, then it is almost certainly too late to rescind it. To rescind an item that has been adopted, there must be a second to the motion and a two-thirds vote in favor of rescinding it.

Reconsider

A group can also reconsider a motion, allowing group members to bring the motion up again at a later date for a second look. This can also take place after a motion has been acted on, but it does require a second. To reconsider a motion requires a majority vote, and it can be debated. Another item of note regarding a motion to reconsider is that it must be made by a member of the group who originally voted for the motion to pass. When a motion to reconsider is made, then any action that is pending for the original motion is halted until further notice.

Motions can be made after or during discussions to accomplish certain goals. A table from the fourth edition of Robert's Rules that outlines the various steps that can be taken for specific actions is listed here:

"Immediately after the table is a brief statement of the differences between the motions placed under each object, and of the circumstances under which each should be used. They include all the Subsidiary Motions, which are designed for properly disposing of a question pending before the assembly; and the three motions designed to again bring before the assembly a question that has been acted on or laid aside temporarily; and the motion designed to bring before another meeting of the assembly a main question which has been voted on in an unusually small or unrepresentative meeting. Motions, as a general rule, require for their adoption only a majority vote — that is, a majority of the votes cast, a quorum being present; but motions to suppress or limit debate, or to prevent the consideration of a question, or, without notice to rescind action previously taken, require a two-thirds vote. The figures and letters on the left in the list below correspond to similar figures and letters in the statement of differences further on. The figures to the right in the list refer to the sections where the motions are fully treated."

THE COMMON MOTIONS CLASSIFIED ACCORDING TO THEIR OBJECTS	
(1) To Modify or Amend.	
(a) Amend	33
(b) Commit or Refer	32
(2) To Defer Action.	
(a) Postpone to a Certain Time	31
(b) Make a Special Order (2/3 Vote)	20
(c) Lay on the Table	28
(3) To Suppress or Limit Debate (2/3 Vote)	
(a) Previous Question (to close debate now) (2/3 Vote)	29
(b) Limit Debate (2/3 Vote)	30
(4) To Suppress the Question.	
(a) Objection to Its Consideration (2/3 Vote)	23
(b) Previous Question and Reject Question	29
(c) Postpone Indefinitely	34
(d) Lay on the Table	28
(5) To Consider a Question a Second Time.	
(a) Take from the Table	35
(b) Reconsider	36
(c) Rescind	37

THE COMMON MOTIONS CLASSIFIED ACCORDING TO THEIR OBJECTS	
(6) To Prevent Final Action on a Question in an Unusually Small or Unrepresentative Meeting	
(a) Reconsider and have Entered on the Minutes	36

The following is also a list of main and unclassified motions that are listed in Robert's Rules that often come up as well.

"Two main motions (to rescind and to ratify) and several motions which cannot conveniently be classified as either main, subsidiary, incidental, or privileged, and which are in common use, are hereafter explained and their privileges and effects given. They are as follows:"

MAIN AND UNCLASSIFIED MOTIONS	
Take from the Table	35
Reconsider	36
Rescind	37
Renewal of a Motion	38
Ratify	39
Dilatory, Absurd, or Frivolous Motions	40
Call of the House	41

Discussing

Discussion on an amendment or a motion proceeds according to an exceedingly specific set of rules that are designed to allow all persons to participate in the discussion. This is the part of Robert's Rules that does the most good for an assembly seeking to give equal rights in the decision making process. First rights to speak go to the person who brought the motion or subsidiary motion before the assembly. Except in awfully small groups, persons who wish to speak after this must rise and request the floor. The chair then grants the floor to persons requesting it in accordance with the order in which they requested it. Each person in the assembly can speak twice on any main motion and its subsidiary motions. No speech can last longer than ten minutes. Also, no one may speak for a second time until all persons have had a chance to speak. Robert's Rules also describe the tone and decorum to be found in these speeches. Debate must be on topic and courteous without any name-calling or personal slander. If the chair believes a speaker is not being courteous, that person can be declared out of order and denied his or her chance to speak.

Consent Agenda Items

In some cases, items that appear on agendas are routine business and so do not need to be considered for full discussion. These items are called consent agenda items and are packaged together for one vote by the assembly. More often than not, these items do not need to have additional actions taken, though, if one member of the group requests an item be pulled from the consent agenda, it is then placed on the regular agenda and treated as an agenda item with full discussion and motions made.

Dilatory Tactics Used by Members

Dilatory tactics are a big "no" in meetings, but sometimes members of the group might try to use them to delay votes.

In this case, the presiding officers must prevent this from happening by noting that the motion was "hostile" and is being ruled out of order. Members who use these tactics can be officially ignored, as they are disrupting the meeting process.

Call for the Vote

When it appears that debate has ended, it is then the job of the chair to move from discussion to voting. This is done by calling for the vote. First, the chair asks the assembly if it is ready for the question. Those present give their assent, or anyone still wishing to speak on the issue can present themselves to the floor at that time. If all have spoken their peace, the chair then restates the question and calls for the vote. Voting is then done according to the following processes, and the chair announces the result by saying that the motion carries or motion fails.

How to Vote, Tabulate, and Determine if a Motion Carries

There are several standard practices for how voting is done. More extensive and private practices have been described in the election section previously. These may, if the assembly decides or if the bylaws dictate, be used for general voting as well. In the absence of a preset method of voting, any member of the assembly can request a vote be done in a specific manner. Frequently, the chair will call for the vote in a specific format, but this can be changed with a request or motion from a member of the assembly to vote in another. The three common ways that assemblies vote on regular motions are by 1) voice, 2) rising, or 3) show of hands. The standard basis for determining a voting result is a majority vote. There are certain instances when a simple majority is not enough and a two-third majority is necessary (or other percentages). In the event of a tie, the chair always casts the deciding vote.

- **General Consent Voting** — This type of voting implies that everyone is in agreement, and the presiding officer might note, "If everyone is in agreement..." and the vote is done. On big-ticket issues, this is not advised, as you do not want someone coming back later with a problem. Take note also that it takes only one voting member to request an actual vote, and then the presiding officer has to follow proper procedure giving the motion and taking the official vote.

- **Voting by Voice** — This is also called viva voce and is the type of vote that is most often used for practical voting purposes. When there is a need for a two-thirds majority vote, this is not the most advised way to vote. Although voice voting is normally accurate, it can still be confusing, and a two-thirds vote of confusion is not recommended. After the members have made their voice vote, the presiding officer announces if the item was adopted or not. If a member of the group does not agree with what the presiding officer states, then he or she can request a recount.

- **Voting by Rising** — When a rising vote is necessary, then the members of the group stand up to vote either for or against a motion. The presiding officer would call for those in favor to rise, and that vote is counted. He or she would then have those members sit down and ask for those opposed to rise. This is by and large a vote that is done when an earlier vote is being disputed.

- **Show of Hands** — When voting by a show of hands, which is regularly how small groups handle voting procedures, the results are obvious in most cases. When hands are used, everyone normally is able to see everyone else who voted, so questions are minimal about who voted in what way. The presiding officer might say, "Those voting in favor raise your hand" and then, "Those opposed raise your hand."

- **Ballot Voting** — This type of voting is done when the group voting wants its votes to be done in secret. This is more often than not done on paper, and the secretary should have the appropriate supplies if a paper vote is called.

- **Roll-Call Vote** — A roll-call vote is when each member gives his or her vote out loud so that it can be recorded appropriately in the meeting minutes. This type of vote is needed only when the voting group answers to another group of people, like the U.S. Senate, for example. The presiding officer officiates this vote and then has the secretary, or another person who can do it, call the roll of those members who are voting. The presiding officer votes last. A person can vote in one of four ways, either: yes, no, abstain, or pass. If a person does pass, he or she still has the chance to vote before the results are tabulated.

Other Voting Matters

Proxy voting and absentee voting are possible if allowed by the bylaws. Neither of these types of voting are acceptable parliamentary voting procedures.

- **Absentee Voting** is when a person votes either through the mail or by a proxy vote (see below). This must be noted as acceptable voting in the bylaws.

- **Proxy Voting** is when the power of attorney is given to another member in order for that member to vote for the absent person during the meeting and vote taking process. Again, this must be noted as acceptable procedure in the bylaws.

Some votes require two-thirds, although others require just a majority. This can get confusing too if you are not sure of what number to begin with in the first place. A majority vote essentially means more than half of the vote, in other words, more than a tie vote.

Some motions require a two-thirds vote. As noted in the fourth edition of Robert's Rules, "There has been established as a compromise between the rights of the individual and the rights of the assembly the principle that a two-thirds vote is required to adopt any motion that suspends or modifies a rule of order previously adopted; or prevents the introduction of a question for consideration; or closes, or limits, or extends the limits of debate; or limits the freedom of nomination or voting; or closes nominations or the polls; or deprives one of membership or office. It will be found that every motion in the following list belongs to one of the classes just mentioned."

MOTIONS REQUIRING A TWO-THIRDS VOTE	
Amend (Annul, Repeal, or Rescind) any part of the Constitution, By-laws, or Rules of Order, previously adopted; it also requires previous notice	68
Amend or Rescind a Standing Rule, a Program or Order of Business, or a Resolution, previously adopted, without notice being given at a previous meeting or in the call for the meeting	37
Take up a Question out of its Proper Order	22
Suspend the Rules	22
Make a Special Order	20
Discharge an Order of the Day before it is pending	20
Refuse to Proceed to the Orders of the Day	20
Sustain an Objection to the Consideration of a Question	23
Previous Question	29
Limit, or Extend the Limits, of Debate	30
Extend the Time Appointed for Adjournment or for Taking a Recess	20
Close Nominations [26] or the Polls	25
Limit the Names to be Voted for	
Expel from Membership: it also requires previous notice and trial	75
Depose from Office: it also requires previous notice	
Discharge a Committee when previous notice has not been given	32
Reconsider in Committee when a member of the majority is absent and has not been notified of the proposed reconsideration	36

When a two-thirds vote is necessary, that means there were twice as many people voting for the motion instead of against it.

A plurality vote is when it is mandatory that the candidate or issue being voting on, such as a proposition, receives more votes that the item or person that is being run against. The bylaws say that a person or proposition wins by majority (one more than half); for plurality to win the day that too must be stated in the bylaws of the organization.

In the event of a tie vote, then normally the presiding officer breaks the tie. Conversely, it is not mandatory that the chair break the tie. One problem is if the chair breaks the tie and looks to the losing side as if he or she was voting in favor of one thing or another by favoritism.

Electronic voting has also become popular in some meetings and is often used in city council meetings as well. Voting members use a keypad to make their vote yes or no, and the results are seen on a screen by all in attendance.

Chapter 6
Write this Down: Understanding Necessary Paperwork and Reports

Agenda Setting

If an assembly does not have an established agenda or follow the standard order outlined in Robert's Rules, then it is necessary to adopt an agenda at the beginning of each assembly meeting. In all cases, it is the role of the chair to establish and set the agenda at the beginning of each meeting, even if a formal adoption is not necessary. Subsequently, it is also the duty of the chair to ensure that this agenda is followed in an appropriate and timely manner.

Taking Minutes

Every meeting that conducts business in the name of the assembly must have recorded minutes taken and distributed to all members. These minutes must include all actions taken by the assembly. Except in special circumstances, the minutes do not need to contain what was said by each member or the gist of the conversations. They should never include the secretary's personal reflections or opinions on the business conducted at the meeting. After the minutes are recorded and checked by the secretary, the secretary must sign them and distribute them to the members of the assembly. At the next regular meeting of the assembly, the previous minutes should be read and adopted.

Robert's Rules note that specific items need to be included in the minutes as follows:

In the first paragraph:

- Type of meeting (the various options include regular, annual, and convention, among others)

- The name of the organization holding the meeting

- The date, time, and place the meeting is being held

- What officers and members are in attendance

- If a quorum was present

- The time the meeting was called to order by the presiding officer

- Whether the minutes from the last meeting were approved (in city council meetings, this often goes under the consent agenda items voted on at one time with other routine business)

The next part of the minutes will include the following additional items:

- Reports given and the member or committee giving the report. This would relate to what the report was about and what action, if any, was taken.

- All motions that were called and the outcome

- Any appeals or points of orders that were called

- Any announcement and the name of the person giving the announcement

The final paragraph lists the time the meeting was adjourned.

Required Paper Trail

In addition to the minutes, the secretary should keep a record of all reports presented to the body by officers and committees. As an addendum to specific meetings, all motions passed or denied during that meeting should be kept in written form for future reference. These, in addition to the organization's bylaws and charters, should be present at every meeting of the assembly to assist in the flow of the business.

More about Bylaws

Although bylaws were addressed briefly in an earlier chapter of this book, it is worth mentioning again the importance of defining and following the bylaws of an organization. The only way in which bylaws can be altered is when they are put to vote and amended. Bylaws are meant to be tools for successful meetings and not stopping the proceedings or causing confusion.

If you are not sure about your organization's bylaws or do not have a set yet, find a good attorney who can help you with this task. Bylaws should be easy to understand

and organized in such a manner that anyone reading them would be able to interpret them accurately. It is also a good idea to make sure your bylaws follow state rules and regulations, as this will be important for the future of your organization. Each specific part of the bylaws should be able to stand alone for proper interpretation. This will also be a paper trail for years to come as to why your organization and officers made the decisions that were made on behalf of the group. Appendix II gives an example of an outline to create bylaws for your organization.

To change the bylaws in an organization, it takes a vote. It is not a bad idea to go over them occasionally, as some rules might become outdated and no longer usable. When changing bylaws, this is called amending the bylaws or revising them as needed. There is a difference between making amendments and making revisions.

When bylaws are amended, this means that certain sections are changed. It must be recorded that a meeting in which the bylaws will possibly be changed will be taking place.

When a revision is done to the bylaws, this means the entire document can be changed, perhaps rewriting the entire thing or just creating an entirely new set of bylaws.

To do anything to the bylaws of an organization, it should not surprise you that a two-thirds vote must carry the decision. The secretary would add to the agenda items that the bylaws are up for revision or amendments, and this would take place before the new business was begun at the scheduled meeting. It is also possible that voting members or others might come to the meeting with their own version of bylaw changes, in which case, if there are more than three options, the most general amendment is offered first and so on until all the options have been presented.

Other useful terms include corporate charters, touched on earlier in this book; standing rules; and affiliated organizations. Standing rules discuss the housekeeping involved with administering the group. These rules can be changed easily and may also be rescinded by members or amended as needed. In the case of affiliations, most of the time, affiliations are required to follow the parent company's bylaws and regulations unless stated otherwise.

Many people will have an opinion about what needs to be included or changed regarding an organization's bylaws. In this manner, you can have amendments to amendments to amendments and motions and secondary motions, and it could go on forever. Luckily, there are limitations to the amendments. Amendments that are to be made to the bylaws and presented at a given meeting should not go beyond what was mentioned in the original notice, and nothing new can be addressed, either.

When amendments are passed on current bylaws, the appropriate procedure for making the changes is easy. After the vote, the new amendment is in effect and is not longer open for debate, vote, or discussion. To let members and anyone not in attendance know of the new bylaws, a notice in writing must go out with a breakdown of any changes. This explanation should be in simple language that will not be difficult for the general public to understand.

Necessary Reports

Different reports are often necessary for paperwork trails when meetings are held. One report and group that is important but often misunderstood, is the committee. Although we will get into what exactly a committee does in Chapter 10, we will discuss necessary paperwork here. Like officer's reports, which differ depending on the report being given, committee reports represent the official remarks and findings of a given committee. If the committee does not agree, then this report is the report of the majority. Likewise, actions taken in the name of the committee, findings, and any recommendations are discussed in the committee report. Normally, the report is presented to the entire voting body and any members in attendance. As an example, say a committee was given the task of finding out how many cities in the area use green energy and why. Then it would contact 20 or so cities and obtain the results from each city. The report would be the finding of how many cities use green energy and why. Another part of the report might be to note why the cities that do not use green energy choose not to. (See Appendix III.) This committee might also be asked to give a recommendation of whether green energy is a good idea for this particular city or company. This recommendation also finds itself in the report as well.

To present the report, you might want to begin with how you went about doing the job, all the information you found and how you gathered it, and the conclusions that the committee drew with the information it uncovered. Finally, the recommendation would come into play. Be ready to defend your recommendation as well.

CASE STUDY: ROBERT E. HAGER

Robert E. Hager

Nichols, Jackson, Dillard, Hager & Smith, LLP

1800 Lincoln Plaza

500 North Akard Street

Dallas, Texas 75201

214-965-9900

Since 1979, Robert Hager has been an attorney with Nichols, Jackson, Dillard, Hagar & Smith, LLP, originally representing all its municipal clients in the area of human resources and civil service. Hagar has extensive experience in all areas of municipal government, including but not limited to, civil service and human resources, constitutional law, litigation, planning and zoning, open meetings and public information, public works and government procurement, condemnations, economic development, and employment law. He has served or is serving as the city attorney for as many as nine cities and acts as special counsel for another city in the Dallas/Fort Worth area. His professional licenses include being admitted to bar, 1978, Michigan; admitted to bar, 1979, Texas; admitted to bar, 1980, Florida; U.S. Court of Appeals, Fifth Circuit, 1981, U.S. District Court, Northern and Eastern Districts of Texas, 1989; and U.S. Tax Court, 1980. In addition, Hagar holds many professional memberships and civic services and has had many chances to use his knowledge of Robert's Rules of Order.

"I normally use Robert's Rules of Order as city attorney and parliamentarian for city council meetings and meetings of boards, missions, and corporations for municipalities and Texas political subdivisions," Hagar explained.

His initial contact with Robert's Rules of Order came as a parliamentarian for fraternal organizations, and he does believe that it provides a rudimentary structure to public and corporate meetings.

Although Hagar has not used Robert's Rules of Order for teleconferencing or new technology, he has used the rules at for-profit meetings and says they are always useful.

Hagar's favorite rule is motion to amend, but he believes his hardest one to remember and follow is motion to reconsider.

CASE STUDY: ROBERT E. HAGER

"The hardest things for groups to learn is the power and authority of the chair," Hagar said, "and the hardest ruling that most chairs have to make is point of order."

Hagar has also helped organizations adopt Robert's Rules of Order when there was previously no parliamentary procedure.

"I have helped create municipality by charter and ordinances and have adopted rules or modified versions."

As he helps the various cities and groups that he works with, it is not unusual for some members not to know parliamentary procedure. In this case, Hagar said he "explains the sequence of motion and the chair's authority" to that person.

Other rules that Hagar has used is Deschler's Rules of Order. "Some of my clients feel that Robert's Rules of Order are too difficult to master," he said.

ℳChapter 7
Fight, Fight, Fight... Understanding and Dealing with Conflict Through Organized Debate

Understanding Conflict

Humans are prone to conflict. These opinionated creatures care deeply about the things they believe in and do, or else why would they act the way they do? For a leader of an assembly or a member, it is important to keep some of the following conflict mediation information in mind. First, fighting and conflict can be a good thing. It shows where people's passions and energy lie, because individuals get upset only about things they care about on a deep scale. If the group can creatively harness this passion and energy, it will be able to do more, not less.

Robert notes in his book, "The greatest lesson for democracies to learn is for the majority to give to the minority a full, free opportunity to present its side of the case, and then for the minority, having failed to win a majority to its views, gracefully to submit and to recognize the action as that of the entire organization, and cheerfully to assist in carrying it out until they can secure its repeal."

Fighting with Parley Pro and Robert's Rules

One way to describe a discussion concerning an agenda item would be "friendly debate." In debates there are different ways that situations are handled, and Robert's Rules provide a good tool for groups to participate in constructive debate. As with discussion, debate operates within specific rules that monitor length and frequency of speeches, the decorum, and the subject matter. In accordance with the idea of maintaining equality for all members, the chair may even participate in debate within certain guidelines.

Rules of Debate

- You must have something to debate — therefore a motion must be on the table to be debated. No issue can be discussed unless a motion has been made and a second has also been called. Then, the debate can begin.

- No overlapping discussion. In other words, be polite and do not try to out yell or out-talk your colleagues. It is the presiding officer's job to call on one person at a time and make sure that when a person has the floor, his or her time is respected.

- The debate can be a discussion only about the motion that is pending and nothing else. When there is an amendment to a motion, the amendment must be discussed and voted on first. Then go back to the main motion.

- Whoever makes the motion has the right to speak first.

- A person who makes a motion cannot speak against it after he or she has brought the motion to the floor.

- The presiding officer must keep things running smoothly and fairly. Although this person does have a right to take part in the discussion, it should be done only if absolutely necessary. When the presiding officer chooses to get involved in the debate, it is necessary for that person to leave the chair before speaking. When this happens, the presiding officer then gives up the chair, and it passes to the person next in charge. If the person who is next in charge has already spoken in the debate, then that person may not take the chair of the presiding officer, in which case, in goes to the next person down who is in line of authority. When the chair has been given up by the presiding officer, he or she is not allowed to take the position back until after the motion that is being debated is taken care of and the meeting moves on to the next item on the agenda.

Certain items are also undebatable; some have been highlighted throughout this book. Conversely, here is a list of what may not be debated.

- The time to adjourn a meeting

- A recess

- Raising a question of privilege

- Calling for the orders of the day

- Lay on the table

- Questions that were asked beforehand

- Limit debate

When a motion is being debated, the person who made the motion speaks first, followed by anyone who wants to be recognized. No one is allowed to speak a second time until all members of the group who want to speak have spoken. There should never be reason a person speaks more than two times and for longer than ten minutes each time.

Manners During Debate

As noted in *Robert's Rules of Order*, the fourth edition, "In debate a member must confine himself to the question before the assembly, and avoid personalities. He cannot reflect on any act of the assembly, unless he intends to conclude his remarks with a motion to rescind such action, or else while debating such a motion. In referring to another member, he should, as much as possible, avoid using his name, rather referring to him as 'the member who spoke last,' or in some other way describing him. The officers of the assembly should always be referred to by their official titles. It is not allowable to arraign the motives of a member, but the nature or consequences of a measure may be condemned in strong terms. It is not the man, but the measure, that is the subject of debate.

"If one desires to ask a question of the member speaking, he should rise, and without waiting to be recognized, say, 'Mr. Chairman, I should like to ask the gentleman a question.' The chair then asks the speaker if he is willing to be interrupted, or the speaker may at once consent or decline, addressing, however, the chair, through whom the conversation must be carried on, as members cannot directly address each other in a deliberative assembly. If the speaker consents to the question, the time consumed by the interruption comes out of the time of the speaker.

"Disorderly words should be taken down by the member who objects to them, or by the secretary, and then read to the member. If he denies them, the assembly shall decide by a vote whether they are his words or not. If a member cannot justify the words he used, and will not suitably apologize for using them, it is the duty of the assembly to act in the case. If the disorderly words are of a personal nature, after each party has been heard, and before the assembly proceeds to deliberate upon the case, both parties to the personality should retire, it being a general rule that no member should be present in the assembly when any matter relating to himself is under debate. It is not, however, necessary for the member objecting to the words to retire unless he is involved in the case. Disorderly words to the presiding officer, or in respect to the official acts of an officer, do not involve the officer so as to require him to retire. If any business has taken place since the member spoke, it is too late to take notice of any disorderly words he used."

Manners in a debate can often be questionable when tempers flare and people want their ideas heard. When listening to someone take his or her turn to speak, think about how you would want to be treated. When you have something to say, frequently just raising your hand is sufficient to be recognized. In some meetings, such as city council meetings, there might be a call light to push to let the presiding officer, in this case the mayor, know that you would like to be recognized. Etiquette for debate is simple:

- Speak when you have been called on.

- Speak to the chair and make comments toward that position only.

- Do not interrupt when others are talking, and that means no whispering to your neighbor, either.

- If something that is stated by another member is not true, then you can make a note of that to clarify, but it is important that the issue be handled politely. The presiding officer of the meeting does have a right to stop the person who is speaking; he or she should do this politely, and you should respond in the same manner.

- Make your words and comments count.

- Discussion can be done with respect for all parties involved, and the more you do this, the more respect you will receive when you are opposed to an issue in the future. Before you speak, it is also important that you have your points in mind clearly so you do not begin to ramble.

- At the end of your debate points, make your position clear, and make sure that those in attendance know why you feel the way you do.

As noted in the fourth edition of Robert's Rules, "Before any subject is open to debate it is necessary, first, that a motion be made by a member who has obtained the floor; second, that it be seconded (with certain exceptions); and third, that it be stated by the chair, that is, by the presiding officer. The fact that a motion has been made and seconded does not put it before the assembly, as the chair alone can do that. He must either rule it out of order, or say the question on it so that the assembly may know what is before it for consideration and action, that is, what is the immediately pending question. If several questions are pending, as a resolution and an amendment and a motion to postpone, the last one stated by the chair is the immediately pending question.

"While no debate or other motion is in order after a motion is made, until it is stated or ruled out of order by the chair, yet members may suggest modifications of the motion, and the mover, without the consent of the seconder, has the right to make such modifications as he pleases, or even to withdraw his motion entirely before the chair states the question. After it is stated by the chair he can do neither without the consent of the assembly as shown in 27(c). A little informal consultation before the question is stated often saves much time, but the chair must see that this privilege is not abused and allowed to run into debate. When the mover modifies his motion the one who seconded it has a right to withdraw his second."

Here is a list of motions that open the main question to debate, and of those that are undebatable, they are made in accordance with the above principles in the fourth edition of Robert's Rules:

MOTIONS THAT OPEN THE MAIN MOTION TO DEBATE	
Postpone Indefinitely	34
Reconsider a Debatable Question	36
Rescind	37
Ratify	39

UNDEBATABLE MOTIONS	
Fix the Time to which to Adjourn (when a privileged question)	16
Adjourn (when unqualified in an assembly that has provided for future meetings)	17
Take a Recess (when privileged)	18
Call for the Orders of the Day, and questions relating to priority of business	20
Appeal when made while an undebatable question is pending, or when simply relating to indecorum, or transgression of the rules of speaking, or to priority of business	22
Suspension of the Rules	22
Objection to the Consideration of a Question	23
Incidental Motions, except an Appeal as shown above in this list under Appeal	13
Lay on the Table	28
Previous Question [29] and Motions to Close, Limit, or Extend the Limits of Debate	30
Amend an Undebatable Motion	33
Reconsider an Undebatable Motion	36

Robert's Rules to Manage Conflict and Remain on Task

Robert's Rules are wonderful resources to harness the passions of a group and yet keep them on task when it comes to debate. A conscientious chair should always be armed with a strong knowledge of Robert's Rules and not hold back in moderating a discussion that is becoming heated or off topic.

Sometimes, a presiding officer is forced to interrupt the

discussion. Sometimes, this might be necessary to protect you or another speaker's rights. The presiding officer must know when to speak up. According to Robert's Rules, there are also times when a motion can interrupt the speaker. These are:

- Call for the order of the day

- Point of order or call a member to order

- Call for a separate vote on a given issue

- Members' requests, parliamentary inquiry, point of information, call of division of the assembly, and raising a question of privilege

Decorum in a debate is always necessary, and good common sense goes along way in taking steps toward this behavior. Good decorum includes listening to other people and what they have to say just as you would like to have done for you. Look at the issues at hand and not the person who is making the motion or debating the issue (it is not personal), try not to ask or consider what another person's motives might be behind how they feel regarding a certain motion or discussion, and speak to the chair when making comments and remarks and not toward a colleague. It is not a good idea to be personal; use titles and not the names of your colleagues. Finally, be nice and play nice and maybe everyone else will too.

When matters do get out of hand, a disruption becomes the order of the day; the pressing officer must act fast to do something. In some cases, a short recess might be called. In other cases when dilatory and improper motions are brought into play, the presiding officer has some choice of how to handle these things as such.

Often, voters who do not like the proceedings or how a motion is going might use another motion to create havoc in the group. The presiding officer can immediately call this person for the interruption noting that the motion is being ruled out by the chair.

Dilatory motions that are often used include using a motion to interrupt the flow of business with points of order and appeals. There might also be motions or notations that are absurd and do not make sense regarding the business at hand, amendments that take time but have nothing to do with the actual business, gratuitous calling, or perhaps stating that an item is unclear when it is easily understood by everyone in the room.

Just as frustrating are the improper motions that can bring a meeting to a halt. These include any items that are not a part of the bylaws or rules of a company or organization, an unrescinded motion with conflict, trying to bring up business from earlier in the meeting even when it has been voted on and the meeting has moved on — anything that is not pertaining to the business at hand.

When Members Have to be Punished or Ejected from a Meeting

Sometimes fighting can also result in bigger issue when members must be punished. In the fourth edition of Robert's Rules of Order, it notes,

"72. The Right of a Deliberative Assembly to Punish its Members. A deliberative assembly has the inherent right to make and enforce its own laws and punish an offender, the extreme penalty, however, being expulsion from its own body. When expelled, if the assembly is a permanent society, it has the right, for its own protection, to give public notice that the person has ceased to be a member of that society.

"But it has no right to go beyond what is necessary for self-protection and publish the charges against the member. In a case where a member of a society was expelled, and an officer of the society published, by its order, a statement of the grave charges upon which he had been found guilty, the expelled member recovered damages from the officer in a suit for libel, the court holding that the truth of the charges did not affect the case."

Of course, this would happen only in a dire situation, but Robert's Rules do allow for such a situation.

Another situation that is addressed in Robert's Rules of Order that might pertain to fighting or an issue more pressing is when a person is ejected from a meeting. This excerpt from the fourth edition of Robert's Rules of Order allows for the chair to use whatever means might be necessary for expulsion.

"73. Right of an Assembly to Eject any one from its Place of Meeting. Every deliberative assembly has the right to decide who may be present during its session; and when the assembly, either by a rule or by a vote, decides that a certain person shall not remain in the room, it is the duty of the chairman to enforce the rule of order, using whatever force is necessary to eject the party.

"The chairman can detail members to remove the person, without calling upon the police. If, however, in enforcing the order, any one uses harsher measures than is necessary to remove the person, the courts have held that he, and he alone, is liable for damages, just the same as a policeman would be under similar circumstances. However badly the man may be abused while being removed from the room, neither the chairman nor the society is liable for damages, as, in ordering his removal, they did not exceed their legal rights."

CASE STUDY: BILL TURNER

Bill Turner

Mayor or Chief Executive Officer of the city of Ovilla, Texas

www.cityofovilla.org

Bill Turner was first introduced to parliamentary procedure as a member of his college fraternity, PiKA at Old Dominion University in Norfolk, Virginia. Since that time, he has sat on the City Council in his home in Ovilla, Texas (about 20 miles south of Dallas) and currently serves as mayor, definitely having a chance to put the Rules into action.

"Ovilla is a Texas, General Law City," Turner explained. "I have been the mayor for the last seven years. Prior to being elected mayor, I served on the Ovilla City Council for four years, the last two of which I served as mayor pro tem."

CASE STUDY: BILL TURNER

Turner said that sitting on the Ovilla City Council made him much more aware of Robert's Rules of Order and its place in city government.

For one thing, he said he feels that the rules help meetings tremendously with organization, control, and presentation.

"These are important components of any successful meeting," Turner noted. "Robert's Rules of Order provide you with a road map to follow in organizing and controlling a public meeting."

Turner said he has not used Robert's Rules in an online or teleconference situation. He said he would not recommend the rules in an electronic environment anyway, because a common thing that happens with written electronic communication today is that the reader misunderstands the writer's intentions because of his or her own interpretation of the words.

"I dislike using e-mail for this very reason," Turner explained. "I find it to be a very cold method of communication. I will always follow-up important e-mail communication with a phone call or personal contact to make sure there are no misunderstandings."

In addition to his role as mayor, Turner is also a financial planner. "As a financial planner I have conducted many seminars where members of the public were invited to attend. Anytime you have a gathering of people, you will have different personality types in attendance. There will always be wallflowers, and likewise, there will always be others who will dominate the discussion, if given the opportunity. As the group leader, you must be able to take charge and control the meeting, giving everyone an opportunity to participate in the discussion if they so desire."

This too is where his knowledge of Robert's Rules has come in handy. His favorite, though, is "Time limit on speakers. By having a stated time limit, you limit disruptive speakers. You keep your meeting on course and under your control."

As for the hardest rule for him to remember, he said that he finds the process of amending an amendment to be laborious and confusing in all cases. The hardest thing for groups to learn when they begin to use Robert's Rules of Order, he said he believes it has to be the basic rules of procedure.

As a chair himself the hardest ruling that he has to make is, "when or how to cut off a speaker or limit debate without creating a disruption."

CASE STUDY: BILL TURNER

Cutting disruption is important when running meetings, and the chair must know just how to do so that the meeting will go smoothly.

"A few years ago we had subdivision up for final approval of the council," he said. "This subdivision was on the western edge of our community, in a pretty well-to-do part of town. Although the subdivision had met all of our building and ordinance requirements, the residents in that part of town did not want their peaceful oasis disturbed by outsiders. Over 60 residents and nonresidents showed up to show their disenchantment and discourage approval. By law, the council had to approve the subdivision. The developer had met all of our requirements, and the subdivision was going to and has become a fine addition to our city. Despite this, the boisterous attendees demanded to be heard. By using Robert's Rules of Order, giving guidelines of how the meeting would be conducted, limiting speaker presentation time, and sticking with the agenda, this meeting, though lengthy, went off without a hitch. The subdivision was unanimously approved. After the meeting I had several people in attendance compliment me on how I handled what they considered a volatile situation."

Indeed, many times newcomers such as the residents mentioned above might not know parliamentary procedure, but Turner said that is fine. "I let them know that they are out of order, that there is a proper procedure to follow, and if possible guide them through the acceptable process."

In the long run Turner is a fan of Robert's Rules of Order. "I would like to offer the following suggestion: do not get bogged down with the details, keep it simple, and stay in control at all times."

Chapter 8
Robert's Rules for Everyday Life

Why You Need to Know at Least 15 Rules

For almost the last 150 years, Robert's Rules have been the standard by which groups, both non- and for-profit, have conducted business. Because Robert's Rules have become an institutional standard in society, it is useful for everyone to know some of the basics so that you can be an active participant in all the societies that you are a part of, from Parent Teacher Association meetings to a stockholder's meeting. Following the basics, more detail is allowed each rule in the next section.

Five Rules you Already Know

Whether from TV courtroom dramas or your church's annual meetings, you almost certainly have heard of or even used these rules already. Due to the popularity of Robert's Rules and their universal appeal in the management of different types of assemblies, many of you have at least some cursory knowledge of their basic structure.

1. **Call to Order** — How to open a meeting and begin proceedings

2. **Adjournment** — How to end a meeting

3. **Recess** — How to take a break

4. **Making a Motion** — How to get your idea heard by the assembly

5. **Discussion** — How to make your opinion on a motion heard by the assembly

Five Rules Everyone Should Know

Should you find yourself, like poor Robert, thrust into a situation that unexpectedly requires you to lead or actively participate in a meeting, these are five rules you should have an understanding of:

1. **Point of Order** — Think something is happening out of order? Want to use a point of parliamentary procedure to stop someone in their tracks and their particular position along with it? Ask for a point of order to make sure everything is going according to correct Robert's Rules.

2. **Limits on Speeches** — Important for keeping meetings on track

3. **Amendments to Motions** — How to change a proposed motion once it is on the floor

4. **Point of Information** — How to ask a question and get information

5 **Call the Question** — How to call for a vote on a presented motion

Five More Rules all Adults Should be Familiar With

More than just what you should know, these rules are important for behaving like an adult at any meeting:

1. **Quorum** — Why you should, and indeed must, show up to meetings of groups you have agreed to be a participant in — because your attendance counts. It is in reality more than just common courtesy, because sometimes meetings are not able to proceed without your presence.

2. **Abstentions** — When you do not want to vote.

3. **Tie breaking** — How to come to a decision when the group is evenly split on an issue.

4. **Nominations** — How to nominate someone for an office or job (or to nominate yourself).

5. **Personal Privilege** — Want to sing "Happy Birthday" to someone? This is how you do it without disrupting the flow of the meeting.

Extra Credit: Three Rules You Will Use Only When You Want to Show off at a Meeting

These are rules that, although common to the floor of the Senate and C-SPAN, are not likely to be used at your local church committee meeting. Still, it is fun to know what they mean and how to use them.

1. **Lay a Motion on the Table** — Frequently misused to postpone something indefinitely, it is important to

understand this rule's *actual* function of postponing something until later in the meeting.

2. **Objection to the Consideration of a Question** — Think that the issue is not ready to be brought to a vote? You can object to it.

3. **Appeal** — Any two members can appeal the ruling of the chair. This is how you can override the vice president of the United States if you ever need to.

Rules that are Sometimes Forgotten

Often there are times that rules are forgotten. There are about ten that most people forget, whether it be in the heat of the moment or just not maintaining proper decorum. But Robert's Rules are not about dictating. For the most part, if a minor error occurs regarding the rules but does not disrupt the process, bringing it up is a mistake. However, learn these rules, and you cannot go wrong.

1. **Do not make a motion** unless the chairman presiding over the meeting recognizes you. Doing otherwise will make you look inexperienced and foolish in many cases. The only exception is when you are calling out a point of order. That said, you might not be first in your motion, but you will get recognized.

2. **Do not decide that moving to table** something is a good idea just because the situation gets a little problematic. To make a motion to table you have to be recognized, and so be sure to wait your

turn. Sometimes this can be hard, as you want to "move to table" in the moment, but remember just because you move to table also does not mean that the motion is dead. A move to table is to move on to a more pressing motion; to kill the motion is to postpone indefinitely.

3. **Another tabling issue** occurs when a person wants to table something until the next meeting. What does this mean? It means it reality to postpone until another time, not lay on the table. Each term used correctly or incorrectly has a lot to do as well with how a motion is handled from debating it, amending it, or forgetting it. Keeping the terms correct produces more efficient meetings.

4. **Yelling out without proper recognition** from the chair to "call to question" is another misuse that can cause problems. Wait until recognized by the speaker before calling an item to question. When this happens too, it is a good idea to remember that the chairperson can suggest that the motion can be voted on if there is no one else who has anything to say on the matter.

5. **There are some problems associated with reconsidering a vote**. Robert's Rules of Order note that to reconsider a vote is a specific action. If you want to reconsider a vote that was taken from an earlier meeting, the correct term to use in this situation is not "reconsider" but instead either to rescind or even amend. Another problem to consider in this situation is when the chairman allows only

the person who voted against the motion to bring it back up. Any member who voted in favor of the motion can bring it back up and call to rescind or renew.

6. **If you do not have the right amount of information**, then a point of information call is a good one. This means you are requesting information on what is being discussed, and that is all it means. It does not mean you can take the floor and start offering your own information.

7. **A friendly amendment** might not be so after all. It actually means that a person would like to add something to the existing amendment. This is a motion to amend and should be treated as such.

8. **When you make a motion to receive a report** or even to accept said report, be sure it is done correctly. A report is just that and should be acknowledged, and then the group should move on to the next item of business. If a report has information in it that needs to be acted on, then a motion is made only on that specific business and not the entire report. There are certain reports that must be adopted when presented, and this includes financial reports, the standing rules committee report, and the program committee report when relating to conventions.

9. **Minutes must be read and approved** (often at the meeting following), and this makes them official.

10. **Express what you mean** when you say "I so move." When you say something say it fully.

CASE STUDY: FREDERICK J. BARROW

Frederick J. Barrow

Littler Mendelson, P.C.

The National Employment & Labor Law Firm®

2001 Ross Avenue, Suite 1500

Dallas, TX 75201

www.littler.com

Frederick Barrow is currently employed at Littler Mendelson, P.C. as an associate attorney where he advises and represents employers in a broad range of employment law matters, including claims based on Title VII, ADEA, ADA, and numerous state statutes, as well as litigation avoidance. He also counsels employers on the Fair Labor Standards Act, noncompetitive agreements, severance agreements, and employment policies. He responds to charges of discrimination filed with federal and state agencies and complying with federal, state, and municipal employment laws, and he resolves difficult and complex matters effectively and persuasively through mediations or summary judgment motions.

He graduated magna cum laude from Southern University Law Center with a J.D. in 2002 and received his bachelor's degree in marketing at Louisiana State University in Baton Rouge, Louisiana, in 1991.

He does many lectures and presentations and has received numerous honors and awards, so it is no surprise that he is not only familiar with, but also uses Robert's Rules of Order on a regular basis, such as when running meetings for the J.L. Turner Legal Association (The African-American Bar Association of Dallas) and the Credentials Committee for the Democratic Party of Collin County.

"I was first introduced to parliamentary procedure while working as a sergeant-at-arms for the Louisiana Senate. I first used it myself as a primary tool as the parliamentarian of the J.L. Turner Legal Association," Barrow explained.

He believes Robert's Rules of Order help meetings because, he said, "without Robert's Rules of Order, meetings would devolve into uncontrollable discussion. They provide a baseline that everyone understands and provide a sense of fairness when it is time to perform essential functions such as ending debate and calling and counting votes."

CASE STUDY: FREDERICK J. BARROW

Barrow even has the chance to use Robert's Rules of Order in online and teleconference meetings, for example when chairing the African-American Lawyers' Section for the State Bar of Texas. As for other technological advances, he is not sure that electronic written communication is the way to go because there can be miscommunication involved.

"Important discussion should only be handled by conference call or in a physical meeting," he said. "There are too many potential land mines when e-mail is used other than to send information. It is simply too difficult to determine tone or intent of a quickly typed e-mail."

In the case of a person attending not being familiar with parliamentary procedure, Barrow said he makes sure there is a copy of the rules at each meeting. "This keeps everyone on the same page and is a quick way to resolve questions if there is no parliamentarian."

One particular story that he has concerning helping another person learn about Robert's Rules of Order relates to the issue of voting.

"Because voting is the most important thing done at a meeting, the chair must have a great understanding of how to count the votes," he said. "One example is when a member wishes to abstain from a vote (refuses to vote). If a simple majority of the voting members is required, the abstention does not affect the outcome of the vote. However, if a majority of the members present is required, then the abstention is essentially a "no" vote. This highlights the level of detail that the chair must have with Robert's Rules on voting."

Chairs must not only have a thorough understanding of how to vote, but also many other things. "No member may speak twice to the same issue until everyone else wishing to speak has spoken at least once," he noted as one of the hardest things that chairs have to face. "It is sometimes uncomfortable reminding someone that they are out of order."

As for what he finds the hardest to remember when using the rules himself, he said, "whether Robert's Rules of Order prevents the chair or president from voting during a meeting or whether the position can only vote in case of a tie. This is a common mistake, and Robert's Rules of Order do not prevent the chair from voting except in rare instances, such as when there is a general member meeting and a vote is called without a paper ballot."

CASE STUDY: FREDERICK J. BARROW

Barrow's favorite rule is from Section 25, suspending rules.

"There are instances where you must get business done, and the rules could prohibit the completion of that work. The purpose of the rules is to facilitate completion of the work, rather than serve as a hindrance."

Barrow said he believes Robert's Rules of Order do make meetings run smoother every time. "The meetings of the J.L. Turner Legal Association were extremely involved in the board's discussion regarding whether to acquire or construct a headquarters building that would also lease space to lawyers and provide "pipeline programs," he explained. "Because of the great interest, the chair of the J.L. Turner Foundation had to remind the attendees that raising their hand did not give them the floor, and neither did standing while another member had the floor. The chair reminded the attendees that they had to first be recognized by the chair before they could properly speak. The remainder of the meeting was extremely orderly."

Although Robert's Rules might be hard to remember and not always to each person's liking, it is still an organized way to keep a meeting on track. "The toughest thing to first learn for someone new to the rules is that a member must first be recognized by the chair in order to speak," Barrow said.

Chapter 9
Cross the Ts: Understanding Occasional Usage Rules and Procedures

You Should Know...

People without a firm grasp of the actual Robert's Rules have developed a group of pseudo rules. This only reinforces why it is important to educate all members of your society in the proper usage of Robert's Rules and to designate a parliamentarian. This book has covered some of this information so far, but this section will cover a list of specific items commonly misused.

Removal by Trial

Sometimes the people whom you choose to lead your society turn out not to be the people that you thought they were. It is a hard thing to undergo, but if you do not know the process of removing someone from office, it is far too easy for a well-organized democratic society to quickly become a tyranny. When this happens, the purpose for which the society was organized is quickly lost. Friendships are broken and feelings are hurt as people resort to whispering instead of voicing their displeasure. Stop this sort of action by having a procedure set in place for the removal of ineffective leadership. Here are some examples of the least you need to do.

You need to determine if the time is right to remove a person from office. Unfortunately, even presiding officers or other members of the governing body can become corrupt and need to be disciplined or removed. In some instances, the chair refuses to allow motions because they do not further his or her personal agenda. If so, this is a violation of the bylaws and needs to be addressed. Here are some options to start to remove or call the problem to action.

To get a person out of office, it needs to be stated in the bylaws how to remove a person, and it needs to clarify exactly what he or she needed to be doing to get himself or herself removed. That said, you can remove any officer as long as there is a two-thirds vote to do away with the person. This is not always easy, though, because that person in charge is bound to have a few friends sitting in the place of power with him. You can also remove an officer with just a majority vote, as long as you have given notice that this will be done and the membership is in agreement with you.

The act of removing an officer is in actuality just the same as making a motion to rescind or to make an amendment to an existing amendment. It is not hard, but you have to have the votes, as you are amending what has already been put in place.

When you find the need to discipline a member, use the bylaws as your backup in this situation. You will need to make a list of all the things that the person you want to remove has done — the various offenses and how you handled these problems as you went along. In some cases, your bylaws might not note the specific reasons you can get rid of a person.

Sometimes, people will act out of order and out of control right in front of everyone, and then you can easily have them removed due to their behavior. You will, though, still need to go through the formal process of removal.

For issues that pertain to facts that you are not certain of, you will need to check out the stories to be sure what you are being told is accurate. One thing you might consider is putting a committee on the person and the situation at hand and having the committee uncover the actual story. It will need to make a thorough report to you of the findings before you officially bring charges against the person you want removed from office or from the membership. In this case, it is fine to say that a committee will be elected to investigate the person's actions in question and if found to be accurate, the person will be removed from the organization.

An individual should never be asked or allowed to make a case against another person; a group of people are much more likely to come to a fair conclusion that can be adhered to by all. When the committee, who takes its time finding the conclusion to assure accuracy, does have a report of findings, then it will present the findings to the membership and either offer a charge against the person in question or make a statement that the accusation was found to be not true.

When the accusations are found to be true, then a trial is set to make the formal charge against the person in question. Decisions need to be made as to how the problem will be handled. At the least, the following must noted:

- The date and time of the trail, with time for the person to make a case for himself and or to find people who will also speak on his behalf

- Who will be at the trial and taking part in the proceedings

- What the charges against the person essentially are and what happened to violate the terms of the membership

- Who will be stating a case against the person on trial

- The letter to the member letting him or her know of the trial and giving him or her the time and place to appear and clarify what the charges are that have been brought against him or her

When the trial is held there are also certain procedures that need to be followed:

- The person to be removed from the organization is allowed to have another person there to speak on his or her behalf. This would be an attorney unless otherwise noted and everyone agrees it does not have to be a practicing attorney.

- Witnesses can be called by the person being accused.

- The witnesses do not necessarily have to be members of the organization but can be anyone that the person charged wants to speak on his or her behalf. One note here is that the person not in the membership may not be allowed to stay for the entire trial, just his or her part in it.

The trial is, in essence, the same as an executive meeting and is opened as such with the presiding chair calling the meeting to order. Because it is an executive session, the meeting is therefore held in secret and is not allowed to be discussed outside the immediate membership. After the secretary reads the necessary resolutions and handles the other business, the presiding officer then announces who is bringing the charges up against the person being accused. After this, the details are explained as to what the charges are, and the person who is being charged says whether he or she is or is not guilty. If the person being charged declares that he or she is guilty, then that is the end of the preceding. In the case that the person declares his innocence, the following steps are applied: opening statements, witness testimony, witness rebuttal, and closing arguments.

When it is time to call the vote to determine if the person is guilty or not guilty, it is handled the same way that any motion would be taken care of in a meeting. If the person is found not to be guilty, then all is well, but in the case that the person is found guilty, then the next step is to decide on the punishment that is to be handed to the accused.

As noted in the fourth edition of Robert's Rules of Order,

trials are serious business, and every deliberative assembly has the right to get rid of problem members.

"Every deliberative assembly, having the right to purify its own body, must therefore have the right to investigate the character of its members. It can require any of them to testify in the case, under pain of expulsion if they refuse.

"When the charge is against the member's character, it is usually referred to a committee of investigation or discipline, or to some standing committee, to report upon. Some societies have standing committees whose duty it is to report cases for discipline whenever any are known to them.

"In either case, the committee investigates the matter and reports to the society. This report need not go into details, but should contain its recommendations as to what action the society should take, and should usually close with resolutions covering the case, so that there is no need for any one to offer any additional resolutions on it. The ordinary resolutions, where the member is recommended to be expelled, are (1) to fix the time to which the society shall adjourn; and (2) to instruct the clerk to cite the member to appear before the society at this adjourned meeting to show cause why he should not be expelled, upon the following charges which should then be given.

"After charges are preferred against a member, and the assembly has ordered that he be cited to appear for trial, he is theoretically under arrest, and is deprived of all the rights of membership until his case is disposed of. Without his consent no member should be tried at the same meeting at which the charges are preferred, excepting when the charges relate to something done at that meeting."

The fourth edition also notes, "At the appointed meeting what may be called the trial takes place. Frequently the only evidence required against the member is the report of the committee. After it has been read and any additional evidence offered that the committee may see fit to introduce, the accused should be allowed to make an explanation and introduce witnesses, if he so desires. Either party should be allowed to cross-examine the other's witnesses and introduce rebutting testimony. When the evidence is all in, the accused should retire from the room, and the society deliberate upon the question, and finally act by a vote upon the question of expulsion, or other punishment proposed. No member should be expelled by less than a two-thirds vote, a quorum voting. The vote should be by ballot, except by general consent. The members of the committee preferring the charges vote the same as other members."

Removing the Public

In some instances, meetings will be held in public, and nonmembers in the audience will disrupt the meeting and need to be removed. The presiding officer has the right to remove any person in the meeting who is acting out of turn and being disruptive. If the presiding officer does ask a person in the audience to leave, a member of the voting committee can make an appeal that the person is allowed to stay. At this point, it will be put to a vote or commonly decided by the voting members as to whether the disruptive person is allowed to stay. If the dismissal of a person is decided, then the presiding chair can decide how that should be done, whether it is being escorted out by the police or the person politely leaving after being asked to remove himself or herself from the meeting room.

Conventions and Delegates: Special Assemblies

The United States Presidential elections are an example of a misunderstood action of conventions, specifically referring to both the Democratic and the Republican National Conventions and the electoral process as well. This example will be used to help understand how conventions and delegates work. Conventions are (in Robert's Rules) special assemblies of delegates chosen by their local representation for that purpose. This is where the House of Representatives and the Congress come from – they are permanently standing, ongoing, professional conventions.

There are always opening ceremonies at conventions, but three more procedures are always necessary, which are as follows:

1. **Adopting the Report from the Credentials Committee** — The Credentials Committee and its report decide how many members are at the convention as noted by registration at the beginning of the meeting. This number will then determine what the quorum number will be, and this number is normally listed in the bylaws.

2. **Adopting the Convention Rules** — These rules are

special rules that allow or disallow for things such as the time a person can give a speech or the length of a report that is given. When a motion on these special rules is made, there does not need to be a second in order for the adoption of the convention rules to be made official. A two-thirds vote is required, and then the chairperson states that the rules are adopted.

3. **Adopting the Agenda** — This is when the agenda is adopted for the meeting, and it is also the time that the members or the delegates would make suggested amendments by motions.

It is also necessary to make a note that the credentials report should be given at the beginning of the convention. If this is done while the registration process is still going on, then the report is officially called a preliminary report. After registration has closed, then the official credentials report is given and adopted, done by the normal means of a motion.

During conventions, motions, resolutions, and announcements must be presented in writing and signed, and only the resolves of the resolution are to be discussed.

Debate is also limited to just two minutes, and speakers are not allowed to speak more than two times, with the second after all members who wish to speak have spoken at least one time.

Agendas for conventions are much the same as regular meeting agendas, with the exception of the credentials report, convention rules, convention program, and often, the various elections that need to be had, including for the officers, auditor, executive board, and committee members.

Sending Delegates to Conventions

Delegates are sent to convention to represent members who are not attending the meeting. A convention is made up of many meetings but what could be called only one session. The delegate who attends this meeting should understand what the members he or she is representing want, thus giving him or her an idea of how he or she will be voting on certain issues. After the convention the delegate then goes back to those members he or she was representing and lets them know the final outcome of the meeting.

Also at conventions there are several committees that are formed. They include:

1. **Credentials** — This committee determines who will be allowed to vote during the actual meeting.

2. **Rules** — This committee will determine what set of rules the group as a whole will follow.

3. **Program** — This committee is responsible for how the business during the meeting will be conducted.

4. **Resolutions** — This is the group that will determine what resolutions will be brought before the assembly.

Each of these committees is important and necessary. For example, the credentials committee's responsibility makes a big difference in the knowledge pertaining to attendance and even how a quorum will be named.

The rules committee has an important function in that the actual rules are determined here as for the convention. Some items that might be addressed in the rules committee is if cell phones are allowed, how nominations and elections will be conducted, how long individuals can speak, how to replace a delegate, and how to approve minutes. These are just a few of the many rules that this committee might be responsible for naming.

The program committee takes its cue from the rules committee and moves into action with the order of business, a schedule for the meetings to be held, and even what needs to be addressed concerning any special events.

Finally, the resolutions committee is important in that it is the gatekeeper as to what resolutions will even be discussed during the convention. This committee in some cases may begin motions and change small words in resolutions without the creator's permission. If this group is chosen correctly, it can also save much time during the actual business meetings that surround the convention.

Also, for successful conventions it is important for members to remain flexible and be open to brief meetings and information sessions in which controversial issues are discussed — and resolved in some cases.

Timekeepers are also important, as time limits on speeches are mandatory. Timekeepers keep a meeting flowing during and should be in plain view of the person presiding over the meeting and each person speaking.

Love this Stuff? How to Become a Parliamentarian...

Believe it or not, parliamentarians have their own deliberative assembly. Professional parliamentarians, and learned nonprofessionals, make up the National Association of Parliamentarians. If you love the intricacies of Robert's Rules, it is possible to make a living helping organizations, especially large public companies, manage their meetings according to Robert's Rules.

Parliamentarians are important when it comes to meetings, as they advise the chairperson on all things "parliamentarian." Someone in the meeting needs to know parliamentary procedure, and it is this person's role to know it and make sure everyone stays on track.

Although this person might be hired for this job, it is also common to vote someone into this position. Of course, it should be a person who knows parliamentary procedures, and this person must also be impartial, meaning willing to pass on any right to vote (with the exception of a ballot, and then the person can vote anonymously).

CASE STUDY: KAY WIGGS

Kay Wiggs

City of Red Oak, Texas, City Council and misc. commissions and boards

Kay Wiggs used Robert's Rules of Order when she served on the City Council for Red Oak, Texas, and also when serving on both the zoning board and the parks and recreation board. She says she also used the rules while on the board of a nonprofit outreach organization, all the time building what she had previously learned into more experiences and lessons.

CASE STUDY: KAY WIGGS

Finally, on the City Council for five years, Wiggs was also mayor pro tem for two years.

"I learned at the start that using parliamentary procedure was a good idea," she said. "I learned by copying what others did. I asked the city administrator for a copy of Robert's Rules of Order when I was made chairman of the Parks and Recreation Board. As I got more into the running of the city, I needed more information on how to account for my actions and why I did them."

Wiggs said that although Robert's Rules of Order are still being used all the time, she believes that some people who use them do not even know what the rules are or the basis of what they represent.

"These rules have been around so long they just seem to be part of the governing system," she said. "We do many things a certain way and do not know why. I feel Robert's Rules of Order are one of those procedures that are a lot of common sense. We just forget them when things get hot."

When Wiggs was on the City Council in Red Oak she says the city went to what was called home rule.

"The difference between Robert's Rules of Order and home rule, to be basic, is that Home Rule cities have a tendency to keep things simple so you can change them and add to them. Home Rule cities can not change things that have been written in their charter without a vote of all the citizens. For most cities that would be either three or more years at the general election for a vote. That would also include all the promotion to get the facts out to the people for the change in the rules. As you know, that can be costly."

Wiggs said that when the city she was working with did go to Home Rule, Robert's Rules of Order were not used.

"The city wrote their own rules, but Robert's Rules of Order was used as a guide. There were some of the old school who never did understand that it was a guide and not a hard and fast rule on all procedures. I think Robert's Rules of Order is a great guide and a very helpful source of information to anyone in the position like I was in on the City Council — especially when you want to help and do the right thing but you do not know how to go about it."

The most upsetting time for Wiggs with using parliamentary procedure was when

CASE STUDY: KAY WIGGS

the city did go to Home Rule versus Robert's Rules of Order and the city administrator and one of the council members never agreed on anything.

"It was with procedures for public hearings," she noted. "One of our council members would quote Robert's Rules of Order the Order number and page, then our city administrator would say, 'We are a home rule city.' The rule we were discussing was when a person could talk and how long and if the council could answer the question and if we had the right to make a decision on the matter right then. Then our attorney would proceed and tell us we use Robert's Rules of Order as a guide only and we do not have to follow them."

Wiggs says that like everything in politics, even Robert's Rules of Order could and did get used for personal reasons and agendas.

"If it could help get a person's point across it was used," Wiggs noted. "I do believe that Robert's Rules of Order help when you are new to things, as it is always great to have a guide to help you understand procedures. Also, when someone questions you about why you tell another person they can not speak it is always a great way to tactfully make your statement."

Wiggs said when dealing with citizens who opt to serve on councils, you get people from all walks of life: business, law, medical, housewives, and students. Not everyone has knowledge on how to be involved in parliamentary meetings.

"When you just go on your own, people get mad, and there has to be a way to handle those people without it getting out of hand. One of the most helpful things for me was learning why we use certain procedures. When I was working on the Council, some of the things that came up could not be discussed in open forum, and Robert's Rules of Order gave me clues on how to handle the audience with the least amount of resistance."

Chapter 10
Understanding Concluding Procedures and How to End Meetings on Time

Good Leadership Keeps Any Group on Task

Along the way, pointers have been presented on how to keep groups moving forward with their tasks. One of the reasons for choosing a presiding officer, as stated in the chapter on elections, should be based on his or her ability to preside and lead a group. If you find yourself in the role of presiding officer, and, like Robert, are a little lost, there are some specific things that you can do that will help you keep the focus of your group. Most important, be it five or 5,000 strong, groups want leaders who step up and take the leadership of their meeting on themselves.

It should also be noted that taking an approach of a dictator in a meeting is not respected nor is it necessary. The chair of the meeting is there to run the meeting and keep it on track, not squelch the other members from making comments or having opposing opinions.

First and foremost, a good chairperson will have qualities of leadership that include:

1. **Integrity** is key because it is important that all members of the group respect the chair and believe his or her actions are not selfishly motivated.

2. **Neutrality** — Being neutral means that no one member of the group should ever feel that this person picks favorites. It is also a good idea for this person to stay out of debates so as not to appear being one-sided in a situation.

3. **Good Judgment** — This person should know when the matter needs to be closed, when a recess should be called for cooler heads to prevail, and when a vote needs to be taken, again in the face of fairness.

4. **Equality** is the most important attribute, as everyone is counting on this person to lead the meeting and call the shots in a way that is beneficial and respectful for everyone involved. He or she should not show signs of annoyance and should always be consistent in making decisions.

Skills that are necessary include:

1. **Good Communication Skills** — This includes speaking and listening and getting one's point across in a fair manner. Remember, each person who speaks believes what he or she has to say is most important. The chair needs to remember this and be respectful of each situation.

2. **Organization** — It is imperative to be organized, because meetings will run only as well as the chair runs them.

3. **Facilitation** — This can also be considered helping the members of the group obtain what they want through understanding their needs. Keeping the meeting going and focusing on the bigger picture is the key to a good meeting.

4. **Ability to Set the Atmosphere** — A chair sets the atmosphere of the meeting by staying respectful to everyone and staying positive. This will go a long way when other members have disagreements with each other.

5. **Ability to Keep People Informed** — It is the chairperson's responsibility to keep things going in a meeting and to make sure that everyone understands what is happening (such as motions). The chairperson restates the motion and then calls for a vote. After the vote is made, the chairperson then gives the result of the vote clearly, for everyone in attendance.

Other areas that a chairperson can take advantage of in order to run a meeting efficiently are: to keep debate to a minimum, to call members out of order without being rude, to keep the meeting moving, to stay on agenda, to prepare for the meeting, and to follow the rules of procedure as necessary.

In addition to a chairperson or presiding officer having a certain set of standards to live up to, it is also important to prepare for the role of chairperson by following the following rules:

- **Prepare an agenda ahead of time with times for each piece of business.** Although it may be impossible to completely prepare for all eventualities that may arise during a meeting, it is important to plan out as much as possible and schedule your meeting well so that you can be accurate when you tell members end times. By making sure that you are on task yourself, you will set a good example for members on how to prepare ahead of time for a meeting.

- **Start on time.** This seems like a simple suggestion, but the number of meetings that do not start on time is amazing. If your members are late and you set a pattern of waiting five minutes for them before starting the meeting, there will be no incentive for them to be on time to future meetings. That said, it is of uppermost importance to make sure you have a quorum before conducting any business (see Chapter 4). If you do not have a quorum, the meeting can still be convened and steps taken to achieve quorum, (call members, wait a few minutes) with the recognition that this is part of the meeting time.

- **Arrive early.** It is impossible for you to start the meeting on time if you are running in the door when you should be assuming the chair and calling the meeting to order. If there are any problems with the meeting space, such as a locked door or chairs not being in your meeting room, there is then no way to avoid being late when convening the meeting. Arrive early, check out the meeting space, arrange the door situation, and have the secretary distribute paperwork so that all is ready when members arrive for the meeting to be called to order promptly at the time scheduled.

- **Come prepared.** Bring all paperwork necessary for the day's business (see Chapter 3 for a list of items a presiding officer should bring to every meeting) and also additional paperwork and supplies you will need to lead the meeting effectively. Pencils and pens are especially necessary and also calendars for the society, personal calendars, cell numbers for members, and other emergency information.

- **Maintain focus with a structured hierarchy.** It may be confusing to think about the order of precedence that different types of motions have in the order of debate and voting, but attention to these details will help you move meetings forward smoothly. If you have the grasp of parliamentary procedure, consider hiring or assigning a parliamentarian to advise you in this area. Often, it is simply helpful for members for the chair to announce the question being considered after every subsidiary motion is being considered.

- **Do not be afraid to call someone out of order.** If someone gets up to speak and goes on about something that has absolutely nothing to do with the question at hand, it is the duty of the chair to interrupt that person and declare him or her out of order. This can be done politely with a gentle reminder of the question being considered and asking him or her to hold his or her discussion. In the same way, if someone speaks for more than ten minutes or repeatedly feels the need to talk, do not yield the floor to him or her.

- **Limit speeches, even in smaller assemblies.** Robert's Rules for smaller assemblies does not limit discussion when there are fewer than 12 members. When leading groups of this size, it is still frequently beneficial to limit the amount of discussion on a particular topic that each member can have. This protects the basic right of each member of the group to speak by preventing one person from monopolizing the conversation while also encouraging adherence to predefined times. In larger groups, assign an impartial timekeeper to notify members who are speaking of their remaining time and when their time is up.

- **Prepare members for business before the meeting.** Before a meeting, distribute agendas and minutes to each member to help members prepare ahead of time for the business that will be conducted at each meeting.

- **Set goals for each meeting.** Although much of the business that will be conducted during a meeting will be determined by the assembly itself, it is important for the presiding officer to set goals with the leadership as to what will happen during the meeting. What will the meeting accomplish? Communication of new activities? Undertaking a new direction? Deciding on things that need to be done? When there is a goal for the meeting, even for regularly occurring meetings, it is easier to avoid slipping into unscheduled discussions on inappropriate topics.

- **Use the commit motion**. If a motion comes to the floor that is not clear or that is creating a large amount of clarification debate, use the commit motion to assign the motion to a committee. Then the committee will do the investigation and discussion outside regular meeting time.

A chairperson who knows the rules will go far in making sure that a meeting runs smoothly and is timely. This is also a good way to prove to the group that you are well-suited for the job as presiding officer. Also, never give up the chair no matter what you think about the issue at hand; your job is to preside over the meeting as appointed. Do not share your lectern with other speakers. Make another area the appropriate place for additional speakers to have their time on the floor.

For Group Members: Do Your Part to Get Home Early

If you are a non-officer in a deliberative assembly, it is equally important for you to prepare before you attend a meeting. As a member of a society, you have certain responsibilities to the society. All members should take it on themselves to:

1. Arrive on time.

2. Be prepared for the business that will be discussed at the meeting. If you feel strongly about one issue or another that will come before the assembly, prepare your speeches ahead of time and be prepared with any motions you will want to make.

3. Arrive with any paperwork that was mailed to you, any reports you need to submit, paper, pencil, eyeglasses, or whatever else you need to be productive and attentive during the meeting.

4. When constructing speeches, less is more. Consider buying a book on debate tactics for assistance in developing concise and convincing arguments.

5. If someone else said what you wanted to say, resist the urge to restate their speech. Yes, you have the right to speak twice on every motion, but that does not mean you have to. If someone has already said what you wanted to say, show your consent with your vote. Of course, if that person is not clear or convincing, you may wish to still give your prepared speech.

6. Learn how to request the floor appropriately. This is more often than not done by rising, queuing at a lectern, or otherwise indicating to the chair that you wish to speak on a topic.

7. Familiarize yourself with Robert's Rules so that any motions you make will not be declared out of order.

Sometimes, meetings can become long and drawn out with secondary motions and amendments being made to the main motions before the assembly. This can become boring for members not directly involved in the subsidiary motion process. It is the responsibility of members to remain attentive and patient with the proceedings, even when they do not involve them directly. Under no circumstances should members revert to conversations among themselves, as this may hinder the ability of the rest of the assembly to conduct business in a timely manner.

Group members such as the treasurer or other officers will also be responsible for giving their reports during a meeting. Most will understand the need to do this quickly and efficiently. Even if not every meeting, officers will have to offer annual reports to the members. This is best done in writing, sometimes offering recommendations or just information. Good reports are descriptive and easy to read, with the following information:

1. Office held and officer name

2. Date of report

3. Time period the report covers

4. Description of responsibilities that have been completed by the officer

5. Future actions the officer will take

6. Recommendations made by the officer to membership

The Treasurer's Report

The treasurer's report should receive special attention separate from the other officer reports and will include important information related to the group, with checking account balances, receipt information, how money has been disbursed, and a final balance being the most important.

When an audit is called, it is for the purpose of confirming the accuracy of financial reports within an organization. Sometimes an audit might be conducted by a committee in the organization or at other times by an audit firm specializing in such reports. No matter who does the audit, the main objective is to confirm the financial records are accurate and have not been tampered with and that the current accounting is being done correctly, with change recommendations.

Most organizations will have budgets that they must adhere to, including city councils. The treasurer would make sure the budget is being adhered to while also bringing to the attention of the group when something is not right financially.

Moderating Discussion

Robert's Rules clearly outline the need to have decorum when persons are speaking on an issue. Robert specifically tells members who are participating in debate to:

1. Remain on topic.

2. Avoid slandering other members of society.

3. Be respectful to the chair and other members, especially when disagreeing with them.

Beyond this, it can be helpful for chairs or assemblies to set specific rules, that are accepted by all members, about speaking in the assembly. These are especially useful when leading assemblies of fewer than 12 people, due to the more informal process of debate.

In smaller assemblies, members do not need to rise and be assigned the floor to participate in debate, and no limits are placed on them referring to the length or number of speeches on a particular topic. Unless the society has established its own rules, it can be too easy for smaller groups to be dominated by a few outspoken personalities. Create agreed-on rules within your assembly which moderate such things as interrupting each other and respecting each other. Then post these rules in your meeting space so that people are aware of them. If someone does not abide by these rules, tactfully draw their attention to this fact and encourage them to rethink their statements. Chairs of smaller assemblies should take care to make sure that all persons participating in the assembly are heard. Asking quieter members if they have any comments before closing debate can often do this.

Time limits have already been mentioned, but there are some standard ways to give people warnings of time limits so that they know when to stop. When working with larger groups, assign an official timekeeper who will time and warn speakers of their time limits during debates. It is standard for timekeepers to warn with hand signals or flashing lights at five minutes, two minutes, one minute, and 30 seconds and then to count down the last five seconds. Even with warnings, members may be passionate about their topics and overrun their allotted time. In these cases, it is necessary for the chair to be "rude" and interrupt someone who is over the time limit or out of order. To do this with a limited amount of rudeness, the chair should simply say, "Thank you for your comments. I'm afraid your time is now up." The proper response of a member when this happens is to simply thank the chair and return to a seat.

How to End a Meeting

At the beginning of every meeting, you should have a set ending time. Attention spans tend to wander after an hour and a half of dealing with the same business. When it is necessary to have long meetings that last several hours on end, the chair's agenda should provide for recesses to allow members to refresh themselves. Scheduled recesses and their adherence will allow members to pace themselves. No matter the length of your meeting, be it 45 minutes or four days, a predetermined end time should be adhered to. There are, of course, times when this will be impossible due to the business at hand. When it is necessary to run over, the chair should encourage the use of an adjourned meeting to continue the business at hand at a later date. If a meeting does run over, the chair should make sure to thank the members for their patience and commitment to completing the business, especially in volunteer societies.

Unless something dramatic happens, regular meetings should be limited to their defined ending time so that persons will attend regularly with the conviction that they will be able to leave at a scheduled and reasonable hour. If business is not completed in this time, it may be necessary to call for another meeting to finish the business at a later date. Whether this happens or not, when the business of the meeting is concluded, it is the responsibility of the chair to conclude the meeting. In societies that meet regularly, the motion to adjourn will frequently arise naturally and follow the process described in Chapter 5. If no one moves for adjournment, the chair ends a meeting by asking someone to move for adjournment. This normally happens after the next meeting time has been announced or decided on, because a motion for adjournment always includes the time of the next meeting. This motion should be worded as

"I move that we adjourn until _____," with the next meeting time specified. This motion is then seconded and voted on; it cannot be amended or debated. Once carried, the meeting is at an end.

Using Committees Effectively to Save Time

Committees are often formed in an effort for groups to have certain people go out to do research and then report back when the time is right. Committees also have the luxury of working under more relaxed rules than the formal group. There might also be subcommittees under committees that are given the task to go out and get even more specific information for the body as a whole.

Committees will draw up procedure manuals to use to stay on target. The most important thing to remember regarding committees is they must know what they need to accomplish. The committee's procedure manual should include information such as:

1. Background relating to the committee

2. Any documents necessary for the committee to work and do the task given to them

3. What the responsibilities of the committee will be as it performs its task

4. Who the chairperson of the committee is and what that person's responsibilities will be regarding the task

5. What forms and reporting will be used by the committee

6. Minutes from the meetings the committee holds

7. Any information from past members who no longer sit on the committee

Chapter 11
Robert's Rules in a Wired World

Do They Still Apply?

Yes, if not more so. There are some rules that cannot apply when persons are not meeting in person, but it is even more essential that all participating members use a common rule of order when they are meeting but not physically together. Especially with online meetings that are not held in a real-time structure, it is more important for members to self-regulate and be aware of what is or is not in order when they participate. Using an exceedingly specific rule of order, such as Robert's Rules, best accomplishes this feat.

First, clarification needs to be made of what an electronic meeting is and how it applies to meetings. Whether it is called teleconferencing or some other form of interactive communication, in the wired world we live in, a meeting online, on the phone, or on video is just as acceptable as a face-to-face meeting as long as the procedures are adhered to properly.

It is also important to note that, to be officially used, an organization's bylaws must say that electronic meetings are acceptable for this type of meeting. Even when a meeting will be held electronically, it must still be posted as necessary, and members other than voting members must also be able to join in as if the meeting were taking place under one roof. A quorum must still be in attendance for voting to take place, and a legal vote still has to be made and verified.

One of the hardest items is to make sure that every member who wants to speak is recognized and allowed to speak, just like in a normal meeting. All the views must be heard, and other members must still be respectful and pay attention. Again, no one should be able to speak for longer than the normally appointed time and no more than twice.

Important notes to make group e-meetings work are:

1. How to verify a quorum

2. How a group member lets the chairperson know that he or she wants to be recognized to speak

3. How a vote will be taken and counted

4. The main criteria, or rules, for holding the meeting

Distribution of minutes, creating agendas, and determining quorum become both easier and more difficult in non-traditional meeting formats. Yet, these basic meeting functions become even more important to create meetings in which participants are fully recognized as equals.

Voting, Motions, and Getting the Moderator's Attention when you are not in Person

When using an online meeting space, there is a subtle way to get the moderator's attention through the online interface or by using a private conversation so that you can be recognized. In a teleconference or videoconference, this is done by speaking the moderator's name or title when it will not interrupt someone. Voting online is frequently done via a ballot or roll-call vote. Voting on teleconference or videoconference should always be done via a roll-call vote. The use of these methods ensures that everyone's opinion is heard. On the other hand, voting via teleconference or other electronic means is not necessarily advisable and is often not permitted in the bylaws. If you think this might be a voting system your organization will need to employ, you should consider looking at your bylaws and making amendments to them.

The Pros and Cons of a Wired World of Meetings

There are many pros to the opportunity of using technology to conduct meetings with participants around the globe. From reducing the costs of national meetings where everyone has to end up in one location to quick fixes for problems that can be determined immediately with all the key players involved, working and conducting business in a world that is technologically advanced has its wonders. Think about the fact that more members can participate if they can all call in from their specific location.

The disadvantages are also worth noting in a world that increasingly becomes dependent on machines for communication and communicating. Here are some disadvantages to the wired world:

1. Problems with equipment being used to conduct meetings.

2. It is not as easy to enjoy the camaraderie among meeting participants, as face-to-face meetings is often what promotes this level of communication.

3. Negotiation might not be as easy, because the back-and-forth communication will not translate as well technologically.

4. It will take members some time to get up to speed on how to use the proper technological equipment, therefore there could be some initial stress involved.

5. Members have to be even more prepared when addressing others through video or telephone.

6. It might not be easy for the presiding officer to recognize who gets the floor first or even for members to effectively make motions.

7. Sometimes seeing a person's face when he or she is speaking helps with communication. In the case of telephone or electronic conference this is not possible and is impersonal.

CASE STUDY: RONALD SCOTT

Ronald Scott

Recording Secretary, International Brotherhood of Electrical Workers LV#20

Ronald Scott attends meetings every first Tuesday of each month for the International Brotherhood of Electrical Workers LV#20 and uses Robert's Rules of Order regularly.

He has been the recording secretary for this group, formerly LV #59, for more than 40 years, with at least one meeting per month.

"In 1953 I became a member of the Future Farmers of America Corsicana Chapter Conducting Team. We had local, district, and state contests against other teams using parliamentary procedure," Scott said. "As an apprentice technician we studied Robert's Rules of Order and the proper ways to conduct a business meeting."

Scott said that through the years he has learned that by using Robert's Rules of Order you can have fairness while also accomplishing the business you need to take care of in a well-mannered environment. "It benefits all the members," he said.

Scott said he believes that all business meetings should use Robert's Rules of Order to be fair.

The hardest thing for groups to learn when they start to use Robert's Rules of Order, he noted, is to follow the rules and not fall into bad habits.

"During contract negotiations," he began, "or a meeting where a vote or a new contract is taken, people lose their tempers and are not happy. The chairman and officers have a proper way of accepting motions, calling for amendments, or voting. Robert's Rules of Order help keep order and get business completed satisfactorily for the majority of the members."

That said, Scott does not believe there is a hardest rule to follow. "You use different rules depending on what you are trying to accomplish," he said.

The hardest rule he believes a chairperson must follow is expelling a member for disorderly conduct.

Scott does not have a favorite rule, but he said he believes "the rule probably used the most is point of order. It may be brought up at any time by any member."

CASE STUDY: RONALD SCOTT

When someone at a meeting is not familiar with parliamentary procedure Scott suggests that there always be a Robert's Rules of Order book available. He says his organization always has one on hand and will read the person the rule that applies to the question.

Should organizations decide to use online meetings as a means of communication with Robert's Rules of Order or otherwise, Scott said, "Be very clear with the words you use."

Scott did had some final words of advice. "Buy a book and study it very carefully," he suggested. "Try to become a part of an organization that properly conducts meetings on a regular basis. Practice is the only way to become efficient in conducting business."

Chapter 12
How to Hold Meetings from Remote Locations

Different Ways and Understanding of Meetings

People do not always have the opportunity to meet face to face in a single location. It is important to understand that meeting spaces can be flexible and varied. There are many ways to hold a long-distance meeting, most commonly via teleconference or through Internet meeting spaces. Whenever you are setting a long-distance meeting time, it is important for the chair to take into account the different time zones that people are located in and to choose a time that will be acceptable to all members involved in the meeting. There should also be a concerted effort to create a sense of collaboration among persons meeting over long distances, as this can hinder cooperation if it is not present.

One of the biggest reasons that e-meetings are being held is because of people being located around the globe and traveling often. There are also many reasons that e-meetings are important for business and groups; some issues must be decided on due to time sensitivity cannot wait for everyone to get back to the office. Another big factor is how much it might cost to get everyone in one place, especially if members live all around the globe, which is not uncommon these days.

There are two types of meetings that are defined by Robert's Rules:

"Synchronous meetings occur when participants are in different places at the same time."

"Asynchronous meetings occur with the participants in different places at different times."

Meetings can take place at the same time or at different times when held electronically; a conference call would be synchronous, whereas voting by taking a fax record of everyone's vote would be asynchronous.

Again, it is important to be clear on what your bylaws allow regarding meetings. It might also be possible to amend your bylaws at some point to allow for e-meetings, but the proper procedures must be met and the votes be counted with the majority being the final say on the matter.

Teleconferencing or Conference Call

Teleconferencing is having a meeting where one or more persons contributes via telephone. These meetings may be set up at least 48 hours before the meeting is to take place. The most common and traditional way of having a teleconference is for one or more persons to gather around a speakerphone connected to persons in another location gathered around another speakerphone. There are also many companies that provide call-in numbers with access codes so that all participants can converse together via telephone. In any case, there is some basic etiquette that accompanies the use of a telephone for participation in a meeting. Most basic is to introduce yourself to everyone present, acknowledge any questions put to you, make sure everyone has a set copy of the agenda, and stick to the agenda as the meeting progresses.

Below is a handy guide for how to run a teleconference meeting or conference call:

1. Make sure everyone involved knows the rules of the meeting.

2. Distribute an agenda just like in a regular meeting, and give participants any background paperwork.

3. Decide on what time the meeting will be held and take into consideration that participants will be around the globe. Often, bad times cannot be avoided when dealing with many time zones.

4. Have a backup plan in case technology is not working in one or more locations.

5. Make sure someone is recording the minutes, which will be distributed to participants accordingly.

6. Assure that a form is also sent to each member of the group to sign which records his or her vote. This form is sent to the presiding officer and is considered

official paperwork. Also be sure that the bylaws allow that this type of voting is permissible.

7. Open the meeting with a roll call and have every member present announce himself or herself as being in attendance.

8. Review the agenda and remind members how to be recognized when they want to speak and take the floor.

9. When speaking, a member should say his or her name first before addressing the group.

10. Address members who are being spoken to so there is no confusion, and clearly say what you are asking or noting.

11. The presiding officer should make sure that all members have spoken and should call on those he or she has not heard from during the discussion to inquire if they have anything to say.

12. Make sure you have counted the votes correctly by calling them back for corrections.

13. When the meeting is over, make sure it is ended succinctly and that all members are aware that the meeting is over.

Internet Meeting Spaces

There are numerous services out there that provide Web meeting services, notably **GoToMeeting.com**, which is ranked as one of the best by *PC Magazine*. The use of a system called Skype is cheap and easy and allows for people to talk to each other from around the world at any given time. With technology being what it is today, there are many other Internet meeting space options, so take your time and find the one that works best for you and your organization. Companies will provide orientations to their individual services, but some basic facts remain the same. You can hold a meeting in real time where everyone is present online at the same time, and it provides immediate feedback through a discussion chat room. This might be a good idea for small groups of people, but most likely not for anything that is more than ten people communicating. It would be hard to keep up with everyone's answers, and the questions are even harder to moderate. Even now though, chat room situations are improving, and there are ways to use cameras to be seen and heard. Chat rooms should only be used for informational purposes and never actual meetings, and in the near future today's chat rooms might be the next phase of videoconferencing.

You can also hold ongoing meetings in a collaborative space where persons can check in and read up on the meeting, view presentations, place questions and comments at their own pace, and vote on issues on the table. These are frequently best when persons participating are in extremely different time zones or when the pending questions are not constrained by a schedule.

When chat rooms are used for meetings, all members must be present and accounted for just like in any other meeting. This type of meeting is possibly the hardest as to identifying how members will be recognized, but through careful discussion a group understanding can be made in which everyone is in agreement on the rules. Again, use these rules to get the meeting going and keep in order:

1   Make sure everyone involved knows the rules of the meeting.

2. Distribute an agenda just like in a regular meeting and give participants any background paperwork.

3   Decide on what time the meeting will be held, and take into consideration that participants will be around the globe. Often, bad times can not be avoided when dealing with many time zones.

4. Have a backup plan in case technology is not working in one or more locations.

5. Make sure someone is recording the minutes, which will be distributed to participants accordingly.

6. Assure that a form is also sent to each member of the group to sign, which records his or her vote. This form is sent to the presiding officer and is considered official paperwork. Also be sure that the bylaws allow that this type of voting is permissible.

7. Open the meeting with a roll call and have every member present note that he is in attendance, recording this via the chat room.

8. Review the agenda and remind members how to be recognized when they want to speak and take the floor.

9. Address members who are being spoken to so there is no confusion, and clearly say what you are asking or noting.

11. The presiding officer should make sure that all members have had a chance to say what they would like regarding a topic.

12. Make sure the vote is counted and perhaps have votes sent in via fax machine.

13. When the meeting is over, make sure it is ended succinctly and that all members are aware that the meeting is over and the chat session is at an end.

E-mails

It is not likely you will be holding an actual meeting via e-mail, but there is always instant messenger for people to speak together in real time, and many people use this means of communication. Robert's Rules note that meetings must have simultaneous communication to consider it a meeting, so e-mailing is not following this mode of communication. But there will be times when you will want to e-mail for various reasons. It is also important to note that in addition to Robert's Rules not allowing it, no state in the United States allows for e-mail to be considered a valid way to hold a meeting. This makes sense, as there is no way to deliberate or come together as a group by this means of communication. It will be a long time before the meetings will run as smoothly as those where people can come together face to face, even if it is just via teleconferencing.

That said, e-mail gives people the chance to talk to each other electronically. Certainly, this is not a bad idea for colleagues discussing various motions and amendments beforehand.

Companies should also create e-mail policies that give employees a clear idea as to what is and is not acceptable in e-mail use. When using e-mail for any type of group correspondence it is important to remember a few things:

1   Make sure that everyone who is participating in the meeting will have the e-mail sent to him or her. When you reply to a message that is a part of a meeting, make sure all members are listed. This can often be done by hitting the "reply to all" button.

2   There are also e-mail lists. This list will enable you to involve every meeting participant, as everyone will be on your electronic list and will automatically get all the e-mails you send.

Also, e-mail meetings are likely asynchronous, and in this way you can also send votes via e-mail or fax as allowed in your bylaws.

Videoconferencing

Videoconferencing is meeting through the use of a video recorder, which enables meeting attendees to see each other from a live television feed or something similar. Both spoken and visual means of communication are able to be enjoyed through videoconferencing, and meeting members can be anywhere in the world. To hold a videoconference meeting properly here are some suggestions:

1. Make sure everyone involved knows the rules of the meeting.

2. Distribute an agenda in advance just like in a regular meeting, and give participants any background paperwork.

3. Decide on what time the meeting will be held, and take into consideration that participants will be around the globe. Often, bad times cannot be avoided when dealing with many time zones.

4. Have a backup plan in case technology is not working in one or more of the locations.

5. Make sure someone is recording the minutes, which will be distributed to participants accordingly.

6. Assure that a form is also sent to each member of the group to sign, which records his or her vote. This form is sent to the presiding officer and is considered official paperwork. Also be sure that the bylaws allow that this type of voting is permissible.

7. Open the meeting with a roll call, and have every member present announce himself or herself as being in attendance.

8. Review the agenda and remind members how to be recognized when they want to speak and take the floor.

9. Address members who are being spoken to so there is no confusion, and clearly say what you are asking or noting.

10. Make sure you have counted the voted correctly by calling them back for corrections.

Holding Productive, Collaborative Meetings Online

The use of e-mail, instant messaging, meeting spaces, discussion boards, and teleconferencing can have the effect of overstimulation on a deliberative body. It is incredibly easy to get off track and have too many topics of conversation or deliberation before the body at one time. Also, because most of this is done through the written word, it is important that persons be especially careful of decorum and discussion guidelines so as not to offend others.

Chapter 13
Etiquette & Netiquette: The Golden Rules

Post and Robert, a Match Made in Heaven?

Emily Post on Etiquette and Robert's Rules on procedure have much in common in their basic intentions — and not just the number of revisions that their books have undergone. Both of these cultural icons sought to teach us how to behave civilly to each other and get things done in society. Basic rules that they outline include deportment, saying please/thank you, and waiting your turn to speak. There are several basic pieces of decorum where Post and Robert agree that should govern our intentions toward each other.

First — Mind your Manners

It is always amazing to me how many grown adults forget how to say please and thank you when they are trying to get something done during a meeting. Robert's Rules constantly remind chairpersons and members to be polite to each other, including scripting the chair's language to include "please" or "may" when requesting reports or responses from the body.

Second — Do Not Speak Out of Turn or Interrupt

Absolutely fundamental to following parliamentary procedure is knowing when and how to speak in your correct turn. Business in deliberative societies cannot be conducted when the members are interrupting each other and when they are speaking out of turn on unrelated subjects. Etiquette calls interrupting someone else rude behavior and unfitting for people in refined society. Post's book of etiquette goes beyond this to describe the importance of listening and responding to the correct topic as being part of good manners when participating in any form of conversation.

By waiting your turn to speak and avoiding interrupting another person, you not only show your desire to work together with the other members of your society, you also show respect for your fellow members. Frequently, in formulating a speech for a debate, actively listening to those speaking before you will enable you to create a more convincing argument by addressing their concerns in your speech.

Third — Do Not be Rude

It may seem obvious to some, but in debate or wording of motions, there is no need to be rude or slander other parties who do not agree with your point of view. Perhaps this subsection should be titled "do not be crude." Although anger is a natural part of any conflict, allowing your anger to dictate your behavior by taking over your voice can only have disastrous results.

This is especially important for chairpersons to note. When

leading an assembly, it can become too easy to revert to naming people and speaking against them. Remember some of Robert's original courtesies for chairs and referring to members as members and yourself as the chair to avoid personal entanglements. In the same way, if members insist on slandering others in their speech, Robert declares them out of order and so should you, effectively ending their turn at speaking.

It's Not Robert's, but it is one of the Best: The Golden Rule

Almost every major religion and group around the world shares some basic take on the Golden Rule — do unto others as you would have them do unto you. This is a basic rule that should underline all our interactions as humans, especially when we are part of a committee. This is especially true when working online, where you do not have the benefit of tone or inflection to convey true meaning.

Some Common Mistakes Regarding Robert's Rules

Although some people might believe rules are made to be broken, meetings that use Robert's Rules do so for a reason. If the bylaws say that Robert's Rules are to be used, do not question it, and do not forget it.

Arguing in meetings has no place when it comes to etiquette, but it will still happen. In the case that it does, remember only one motion (or idea) should be on the floor at any one time. Do not start arguing about something that is not being discussed. What about secondary motions? Still, you can consider only one question at a time, even if there are other motions pending. Then you handle each motion in order of importance.

Another good rule to follow regarding acting as chairperson is to respect all the members in the group and not voting impartially or on one side every time. A good leader knows better. If a vote is tied, then the presiding officer might be asked to vote to break the tie; again, showing impartiality to the situation is a sign of good leadership.

Do not say something like, "The parliamentarian said to do that" if that is not the case. It is the chair's final call to make a ruling, and it is not polite to disrespect the final decision.

As the chair, it is polite to ask if there is any unfinished business that needs to be addressed before the meeting is adjoined. This would be motions from another meeting that were not resolved as well as business that still needs to be addressed.

Netiquette for Online Meetings, E-mails, and Instant Messages

Many people do not know some basic etiquette (called netiquette) for how to behave to each other online. Before you have an online meeting, or participate in one, here are a few things you should bear in mind:

Say what you mean in a polite and considerate way. If it will smooth the conversation out to use more words, do so. Wait for someone to respond to your previous question, even if you type at 60 words per minute and he or she hunts and pecks, before you continue the conversation.

Also, in any netiquette discussion never type in all caps as it is considered shouting.

Regarding etiquette for videoconferencing, speak slowly and wait for members to respond, remember there could be some lag time as you are communicating around the world. Do not dress too loudly, and when you have to make noise such as shuffling papers or have other phones ringing, the mute button is everyone's friend.

For conference call etiquette specifically, be on time; take the call in a location where there is not too much background noise; try not to use your cellular phone, as connections are often poor; and do not put the phone on hold if you need to do something else. You would not leave a meeting you were present at any other venue, so do not do it in a conference call either.

ASHA Electronic Meetings

There is another type of electronic meeting procedure you might want to become familiar with called The American Speech-Language Hearing Association (ASHA), and this group has a legislative body of about 150 members who regularly conduct electronic meetings to get their business done. The rules it currently uses were founded in 1999, and by looking at this organization you can further learn its rules, how the meetings are conducted, and how to adapt some of what it uses to your own organization, if needed.

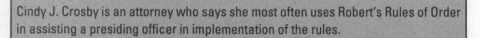

CASE STUDY: CINDY J. CROSBY

Cindy J. Crosby, attorney at law

Bickerstaff Heath Delgado Acosta LLP

816 Congress Avenue, Suite 1700

Austin, TX 78701-2443

512-472-8021

ccrosby@bickerstaff.com

Cindy J. Crosby is an attorney who says she most often uses Robert's Rules of Order in assisting a presiding officer in implementation of the rules.

"I am the legal advisor to various cities and their boards and commissions, and it is important to know the rules when questions arise during the course of the meeting," she began.

Crosby first learned parliamentary procedure by sitting in meetings as an assistant attorney and observing experienced legal advisors in their role as city attorney to cities, boards, and commissions.

"I also learned by reading the Rules and visiting Web sites on the topic when preparing for a meeting and a particular issue may be discussed."

She did note, however, that in her experience Robert's Rules of Order have not helped the meetings she has been involved in for the most part.

"Robert's Rules of Order has not been helpful to most of my meetings and clients, as it is too cumbersome and not applicable to smaller meetings and forums. The rules have not added to the substance of the meeting or ensured that the proper procedure is being followed. In fact the rules often add to the contentiousness of the meeting."

Although she does attend teleconference meetings, she has not used the rules in those meetings because "Teleconference meetings I have conducted with clients, engineers and builders are not conducive to the formalities of Robert's Rules," she said.

Neither does she use them at for-profit business meetings. "Most for-profit business meetings I have either conducted or attended were handled informally,

CASE STUDY: CINDY J. CROSBY

and Robert's Rules of Order were not necessary or conducive to the operation of the meeting."

When Crosby does use the Robert's Rules of Order she says the hardest rule for her to remember as a legal advisor to a client is the actual order of speakers when motions are made and seconded, and when discussion by the board members is permitted.

"I rarely lead or act as parliamentarian for a meeting," she noted.

She said she believes the hardest thing for groups to learn when they start to use Robert's Rules would be to use and follow them at every meeting while also using consistent application of the Rules.

"The group members also have a hard time understanding and relinquishing the floor and authority to the chair," she said. "This last issue may not necessarily be directly due to the application of Robert's Rules but the different personalities involved and desire by politicians and board members to get their message heard. Groups also have difficulty in understanding that the chair can vote to create a tie, and what happens when the chair does or when a motion fails. It is hard for members to comprehend that an item just dies and does not provide any closure in the members' minds."

The hardest ruling Crosby has seen most chairs have to make first depends on the strength and fortitude of the chair.

"They often have problems with controlling the general flow and procedure of the meeting and what to do next. Some can be easily flustered when challenged by a fellow board member or member of the public to either implement the rules or is questioned on a rule. Chairs also have difficulty in fairly limiting the time speakers may speak and often can be selective in limiting certain speakers. Also, as most chairs are not lawyers, chairs often do not follow up to ensure things are on the record. As an attorney it is always a concern that motions are actually voted on, that names of speakers are given, and that when a party nods that the record reflects the physical indication since the audio tape does not pick up when somebody shakes their head."

As for Crosby's favorite rule, "My favorite is the rule that permits a motion to postpone trumping any motion on the table. This can be a powerful tool to a board member who understands the application of this rule and stop further action and vote on a

CASE STUDY: CINDY J. CROSBY

matter. It can stop a controversial discussion and possible death of an item. This can also be a double-edged sword and prevent matters from being acted on. In the game of rock, paper, and scissors, this rule is the "paper" in the game, as it can stop a motion to deny or motion to approve," she said.

Crosby has helped an organization adopt Robert's Rules of Order when it was not previously using parliamentary procedure. "It was approved without question or comment," she noted. "Other times cities have adopted portions of Robert's Rules and added rules of their own. The problem or issue is not in adopting the Rules but in the actual application and implementation of the Rules. The Rules are not a problem until it applies to a member trying to get their item adopted."

However, again, Crosby does not necessarily feel that Robert's Rules of Order help meetings to run smoothly.

"Whenever there is a question on a rule it always brings up multiple interpretations and many of the board stating, 'That's not how it was done at the last meeting,' or at another board they serve on."

Still it is a good idea to implement when necessary, and she says that in cases when someone is not familiar with parliamentary procedure, she does try to help.

"If the lack of familiarity appears during the meeting, as it often does, I certainly do not want to point out their ignorance but try to diplomatically give guidance when I can," she said. "Either before or after a meeting, if it is the chair that is not familiar with parliamentary procedure, I will either try to address the issue with the superior administrative staff member and have them discuss it with the chair or address it with the chair directly and hold the discussion separately from other board members. I may offer to give a training session to the entire board or entity or just to the chair. I may also offer additional resources such as books or links to helpful Web sites."

Crosby has also worked with other sets of parliamentary procedure rules in cities she works with on a regular basis. One such city has a population of more than 500,000 and has adopted a modified and expanded Robert's Rules. Although the basics of Robert's Rules of Order have been adopted, there are also additional procedures for public comment and order of speakers. The rules have also been amended to include the procedure for placing items on the agenda such as deadlines before the meeting and required signatures, she noted.

When it comes to using electronic means with Robert's Rules and the certain miscommunication at times, Crosby advised, "Included in the problem

CASE STUDY: CINDY J. CROSBY

of interpretation of words is the lack of the ability of conveying the tone of a message. In order to avoid this issue, I have had to learn to be much briefer in my e-mails. I feel that the "emoticons" such as happy faces are not professional and will not use them in work-related e-mails. In effort to avoid these scenarios, which I have experienced many times, I have attempted to initiate more telephone conversations when possible, then follow up with an e-mail stating what the conversation entailed."

Although Crosby does not have a particular story to tell about using Robert's Rules of Order she did add, "With most work, preparation is the key. It is too late to learn the rules during the meeting. To the extent possible, not only is it important to know the rules prior to the meeting, but also to discuss potential issues with staff and members of the board that they anticipate may arise during the meeting."

Chapter 14
When There is not a Rule

House Rules

Sometimes, Robert's Rules do not apply to your organization. Perhaps your organization is more informal than Robert's Rules, and you want something that will be easier to use and understand. In these cases, some organizations choose to write their own rules or add on to the way that they use Robert's Rules through creating house rules of order. In these cases, it is important for your house rules to be written down and included in your bylaws if they are regularly used.

Using a "Relaxed" or Modified Version of the Rules

If your organization or deliberative assembly is small, it may be that you can use Robert's Rules in a more relaxed atmosphere. This is dangerous and sticky ground, unless it is clearly understood by all members that in the event of a debate or argument, the entire group will immediately revert to a stricter use of the Rules. Occasions when this works are ones where the chair has a strong understanding of Robert's Rules and their underlying principles and where the group is small (normally fewer than ten).

The Buck Stops Here

When it comes down to it, the chair makes the ruling about the use of a rule, with the advice of the parliamentarian. This can be a heavy burden to handle, but if the rules are handled properly, then it is easier to communicate this to the group.

Parking Lot Conversations

All meetings end in "parking lot conversations," which are regularly where much of the work of the group gets done and planned. These are the coffee-hour chats, the drinks after work, the walk to the car, the review with a supervisor. When the meeting is reviewed, plans are made and people talk about what just happened. You have the choice to make these conversations good ones or bad ones.

The most important thing to remember is never to talk bad about another group member among other members of the group. You can bet it will get back to that person and might come back to haunt you as well. Keep in mind too, that you should never put anything in writing, be it a letter or e-mail, that could come back and haunt you. Being a good group member means being a team player and remembering that a good balance of everyone achieving results is the most important thing.

One of the most important things to remember when using and understanding Robert's Rules of Order is that a parliamentarian is a good person to have on hand, or at the very least useful for information to help you get through the tough times. For those questions that are still unanswered, here are some useful Web sites that might help.

<u>American Institute of Parliamentarians (AIP)</u> — The mission of the American Institute of Parliamentarians is to offer the highest standards of parliamentary procedure. **www. parliamentarians.org**

<u>Rules Used By the United States Senate and House of Representatives</u> — The parliamentary procedure rules used by the U.S. House of Representatives and the U.S. Senate. **http://thomas.loc.gov/home/legbranch/legbranch. html**

<u>Parliamentary Procedure Glossary, Third Edition</u> — A detailed glossary of parliamentary procedure terms and phrases used by the Canada House of Commons. **www.parl. gc.ca/information/about/process/house/glossary/ gloss-e.htm**

CASE STUDY: MONTE AKERS

Monte Akers

Partner, Akers & Boulware-Wells, LLP

816 Congress, Suite 1725

Austin, TX 78701

Monte Akers uses Robert's Rules of Order as the official procedure to be followed at all city council meetings of the City of Glenn Heights, TX, of which he is the city attorney. "It is used as a guide to assist in the fair and efficient conduct of council meetings," he said. "The rules can also provide a solid foundation for debate and discussion at council meetings and can be used quite effectively to promote a fair and orderly meeting. However, Robert's Rules can also be used as a roadblock. In an environment where not everyone knows Robert's Rules, the technical requirements of many of

CASE STUDY: MONTE AKERS

the rules can be used to impede and delay the Council. They should be used as they were designed — a tool — and not as a club."

In the past Akers said meetings have tended to run more smoothly when Robert's Rules of Order were used.

"Robert's Rules and the Texas Open Meeting Act rarely coincide, mainly because they address different concerns," Akers said. "However, both Robert's Rules of Order and the Open Meeting Act require that any debate pertain to subject matter posted on the agenda. Without this rule, many council meetings would turn into a broad-ranging public forum on the state of the city. Robert's Rules of Order and the subject matter constraints on debate help keep meetings often on track."

Akers' favorite rule is, "To the extent there is a 'favorite' rule, it is addressing decorum in debate. Often, debates and discussion can devolve into personal attacks and worse. At a meeting where Robert's Rules of Order are in effect, this rarely happens."

Indeed, some of the rules can be hard, even if necessary, and Akers says the hardest rule that he finds to follow is to restrain discussion.

"It is often difficult to restrain discussion on a motion or amendatory motion currently on the table. In a large meeting, it can take a certain amount of time for all parties to express themselves. Occasionally there is a motion made before the discussion is concluded, and if Robert's rules are adhered to strictly, the members of the council may become confused or be unable to express their concerns adequately. It is at this point that strict adherence to the rules does not promote decision making."

Akers went on to say, "The leader, or parliamentarian, of a meeting inevitably finds it difficult to enforce rules that restrict debate, and again, Robert's Rules were created to assist in the conduct of meetings, not obstruct. If a rule requires the governing body to restrict or stop valid, meaningful debate, the City's interests are not served, even though the same rule may prevent repetitive or redundant debate."

Although the hardest rule for him to remember might be restraint on discussion, he believes the hardest rules for groups is that Robert's Rules of Order entail a certain amount of formalism.

"When groups first learn Robert's Rules, they are usually more accustomed to a looser, informal process. The transition for the old process to a more structured process can be a difficult one."

CASE STUDY: MONTE AKERS

That said, the hardest rule for a chair is, "a difficult ruling must often be made on whether a particular discussion relates directly to the agenda item to be debated. Council members must be given some leeway in order to make their point in a discussion, but at the same time, debate must remain germane to the question pending on the floor."

Akers said having someone at a meeting is not familiar with parliamentary procedure it can also be a problem.

"If they cannot become familiar by watching the council in action, they should submit written questions to the City Attorney about matters they do not understand," he said. "Certainly a member of a deliberating body may pose questions of the parliamentarian — usually the City Attorney — before attempting to make a motion or taking other formal action."

One story that comes to Akers' mind when thinking about how to help a person learn about Robert's Rules and the basic principles of parliamentary law is, "One can compare Robert's Rules of Order to rules in a discussion. When two people are having a discussion, most rules aren't needed, and the two individuals can work out an informal arrangement so that both sides have an opportunity to both listen and convey their side of the discussion. However, as we increase the number of individuals involved in the discussion, any sense of order quickly breaks down. Individuals must choose between cutting each other off to make a point, shouting, or withdrawing from the discussion entirely. As the number of people in the discussion rises above a certain threshold, any meaningful discussion without a set of rules to organize the discussion becomes difficult or impossible. Robert's Rules of Order make such a discussion possible."

Although Akers does use technology, he does not think that e-mails have a place in the bottom-line use of Robert's Rules of Order.

"Misunderstandings can often occur in e-mail precisely because of the lack of formality of the medium," he noted. "In addition, drafting an e-mail can take mere seconds, and the reader of the e-mail does not have the benefit of listening to the tone of voice that the message may have been delivered in. Avoiding this problem requires that an individual simply take an appropriate amount of time to draft a message that is clear and concisely conveys the author's intent."

Appendix I
Notices & Minutes

The notices and minutes used in this appendix are from actual meetings held in Cedar Hill, Texas in 2008. All documents are reprinted by permission.

NOTICE OF CITY COUNCIL MEETING
NOVEMBER 27, 2007
COUNCIL CHAMBER, CITY HALL
CEDAR HILL, TEXAS
7:00 P.M.

MISSION STATEMENT: The mission of the City of Cedar Hill is to deliver the highest quality municipal services to our citizens and customers consistent with our community values.

VISION STATEMENT: We envision Cedar Hill as a premier city that retains its distinctive character, where families and businesses flourish in a safe and clean environment.

AGENDA

I. Call the meeting to order.

II. Pledge of Allegiance.

III. Invocation — City Council Member Daniel C. HaydinJr.

IV. Presentations:

NOTICE OF CITY COUNCIL MEETING

1. Present Certificates of Recognition to Tanya Medina, eighth-grade student, Bessie Coleman Middle School, and Christopher Long, eighth-grade student, Permenter Middle School — S.T.A.R. Student Awards for the month of November.

V. Public Hearing.

1. Conduct the first public hearing to discuss the proposed annexation of a tract of land containing approximately 0.947 acres of land situated in the W. W. Merrell Survey, Abstract No. 876, and being parts of the existing right of way of Wintergreen Road and South Main Street.

VI. Consent Agenda:

Items listed under the Consent Agenda are considered routine and are generally enacted in one motion. Any City Council member may remove any item from the Consent Agenda for separate discussion and consideration.

1. Consider approving the minutes of November 13, 2007.

VII. Citizens Forum.

VIII. Regular Agenda:

1. Consider authorizing the Mayor to execute an agreement between the City of Cedar Hill and Quorum for architectural services for a new animal shelter.

2. Consider adoption of Ordinance No. 2007-340 establishing a 30 mph school zone on FM 1382 in the vicinity of Sims Drive.

IX. Adjourn.

I certify that the above notice of meeting was posted in accordance with the Texas Open Meetings Act on the 21st day of November 2007.

Frankie Lee

City Secretary

NOTICE OF CITY COUNCIL MEETING

This facility is wheelchair accessible. Handicapped parking spaces are available. To arrange for sign interpretative services or special accommodations, please call 972-291-5100 Ext. 1011 or (TDD) 1-800-RELAY TX (1-800-735-2989) at least 48 hours ahead of the meeting.

PREMIER STATEMENTS

CEDAR HILL HAS EXCELLENT, SAFE & EFFICIENT MOBILITY

CEDAR HILL IS SAFE

CEDAR HILL IS CLEAN

CEDAR HILL HAS TEXAS SCHOOLS OF CHOICE

CEDAR HILL HAS VIBRANT PARKS AND NATURAL BEAUTY

CEDAR HILL HAS A STRONG AND DIVERSE ECONOMY

MINUTES — CITY COUNCIL MEETING
NOVEMBER 27, 2007

The City Council of the City of Cedar Hill, Texas, met in regular session Tuesday, November 27, 2007, 7:00 p.m., City Hall, City of Cedar Hill, Texas.

All members of the City Council were present, to wit: Mayor Rob Franke, Mayor Pro Tem Cory Spillman, Council Members Wade Emmert, Makia Epie, Daniel C. Haydin Jr., Greg Patton, and Clifford Shaw.

I. Call the meeting to order.

Mayor Franke called the meeting to order, declaring it an open meeting, that a quorum was present and that the meeting notice was duly posted.

II. Pledge of Allegiance.

Council Member Emmert led the Pledge of Allegiance.

III. Invocation — City Council Member Daniel C. HaydinJr.

Council Member Haydin gave the invocation.

MINUTES — CITY COUNCIL MEETING

IV. Presentations:

1. Present Certificates of Recognition to Tanya Medina, eighth-grade student, Bessie Coleman Middle School, and Christopher Long, eighth-grade student, Permenter Middle School — S.T.A.R. Student Awards for the month of November.

Mayor Franke presented a Certificate of Recognition to Christopher Long and gave him an opportunity to introduce his parents and his principal.

Tanya Medina was not present.

V. Public Hearing:

1. Conduct the first public hearing to discuss the proposed annexation of a tract of land containing approximately 0.947 acres of land situated in the W. W. Merrell Survey, Abstract No. 876, and being parts of the existing right of way of Wintergreen Road and South Main Street.

Mayor Franke opened the public hearing for comments on the proposed annexation. There being no one to speak, Mayor Franke closed the public hearing.

VI. Consent Agenda:

Items listed under the Consent Agenda are considered routine and are generally enacted in one motion.

Mayor Franke introduced the following Consent Agenda item for consideration.

1. Consider approving the minutes of November 13, 2007.

A motion was made by Council Member Haydin and seconded by Council Member Patton to approve the minutes on the Consent Agenda. The motion carried unanimously.

VII. Citizens Forum.

Marseea Carthan, 945 McGehee Avenue, asked the City Council to review the penalty dates for late payments on utility bills. She said she receives a late penalty on her water bill each month, because the bill is due before her monthly payday. She suggested imposing the penalty after the next billing date.

MINUTES — CITY COUNCIL MEETING

Mayor Franke referred her concerns to the staff to review. He suggested that this issue might be considered with the next review of the water rates.

Gary Moon, 306 Cooper Street, asked the City Council to reconsider the conditional use permit for Trios Grill at 316 Cooper Street, because he felt the restaurant's outside music violated the City's noise ordinance. Moon said he had talked with the restaurant owner about the noise and called the police department to complain about the loud music a couple of times. He suggested amending the permit to restrict loud musical instruments and amplifiers outside the restaurant.

Mayor Franke referred Moon's complaint to the staff to investigate and to report to the City Council.

Mark Bielamowicz commented on Carthan's complaint about the late fees, stating he had received a $100 late fee because it took six days to receive the bill from the post office. His primary concern was the mandatory public notice in the newspaper about a violation of coliform found in a water sample. He thought the notice should have been larger due to the serious nature of the issue. He said he had not received a response to his phone calls to the City about this matter.

Mayor Franke stated that such reports are also placed on the water bills.

VIII. Regular Agenda:

1. Consider authorizing the Mayor to execute an agreement between the City of Cedar Hill and Quorum for architectural services for a new animal shelter.

   Mayor Franke announced that the City Council had received a briefing on this item during the briefing session and in previous meetings. He added that this matter is in cooperation with the Cities of Duncanville and DeSoto.

   A motion was made by Council Member Epie and seconded by Council Member Haydin to authorize the Mayor to enter into an agreement with Quorum for architectural services for a new animal shelter. The motion carried unanimously.

2. Consider adoption of Ordinance No. 2007-340 establishing a 30 mph school zone on FM 1382 in the vicinity of Sims Drive.

MINUTES — CITY COUNCIL MEETING

Mayor Franke introduced the item to consider adoption of written Ordinance No. 2007-340 entitled,

"SCHOOL SPEED ZONE LIMIT ORDINANCE: AN ORDINANCE PROVIDING FOR THE ESTABLISHMENT OF NEW LIMITS OF SPECIAL SPEED ZONES WITHIN THE CORPORATE LIMITS OF THE CITY OF CEDAR HILL, TEXAS; PROVIDING SPEED LIMITATIONS; PROVIDING PENALTY OF VIOLATION; AUTHORIZING THE CITY MANAGER OR HIS DESIGNATED REPRESENTATIVE TO IMPLEMENT ORDINANCE BY PLACEMENT OF SIGNS, SIGNALS AND TRAFFIC CONTROL DEVICES; PROVIDING A SEVERANCE CLAUSE; PROVIDING A CONFLICT CLAUSE, AND PROVIDING FOR AN EFFECTIVE DATE."

A motion was made by Mayor Pro Tem Spillman and seconded by Council Member Patton to adopt Ordinance No. 2007-340. The motion carried unanimously.

IX. Adjourn.

Upon a motion by Mayor Pro Tem Spillman and second by Council Member Haydin, the meeting adjourned at 7:22 p.m. by unanimous vote.

_____

Rob Franke, Mayor

ATTEST:

_____

Frankie Lee, City Secretary

NOTICE OF SPECIAL CITY COUNCIL MEETING
JANUARY 15, 2008
BLUEBONNET ROOM
CEDAR HILL RECREATION CENTER
310 EAST PARKERVILLE ROAD
CEDAR HILL, TEXAS

NOTICE OF SPECIAL CITY COUNCIL MEETING

6:00 P.M.

MISSION STATEMENT: The mission of the City of Cedar Hill is to deliver the highest quality municipal services to our citizens and customers consistent with our community values.

VISION STATEMENT: We envision Cedar Hill as a premier city that retains its distinctive character, where families and businesses flourish in a safe and clean environment.

AGENDA

I. Call the meeting to order.

II. Conduct a workshop to discuss the Government Center Facilities Operation and Maintenance Agreement.

III. Adjourn.

I certify that the above notice of meeting was posted in accordance with the Texas Open Meetings Act on the 10th day of January 2008.

Frankie Lee

City Secretary

This facility is wheelchair accessible. Handicapped parking spaces are available. To arrange for sign interpretative services or special accommodations, please call 972-291-5100 Ext. 1011 or (TDD) 1-800-RELAY TX (1-800-735-2989) at least 48 hours ahead of the meeting.

PREMIER STATEMENTS

CEDAR HILL HAS EXCELLENT, SAFE & EFFICIENT MOBILITY

CEDAR HILL IS SAFE

CEDAR HILL IS CLEAN

CEDAR HILL HAS TEXAS SCHOOLS OF CHOICE

CEDAR HILL HAS VIBRANT PARKS AND NATURAL BEAUTY

CEDAR HILL HAS A STRONG AND DIVERSE ECONOMY

MINUTES — CITY COUNCIL SPECIAL MEETING
JANUARY 15, 2008

The City Council of the City of Cedar Hill, Texas, met in special session Tuesday, January 15, 2008, 6:00 p.m., Bluebonnet Room, Cedar Hill Recreation Center, 310 East Parkerville Road, Cedar Hill, Texas.

All members of the City Council were present, to wit: Mayor Rob Franke, Mayor Pro Tem Cory Spillman, Council Members Wade Emmert, Makia Epie, Daniel C. Haydin Jr., Greg Patton, and Clifford Shaw.

I. Call the meeting to order.

Mayor Franke called the meeting to order, declaring it an open meeting, that a quorum was present and that the meeting notice was duly posted.

II. Conduct a workshop to discuss the Government Center Facilities Operation and Maintenance Agreement.

The City Council conducted a workshop to discuss concepts for development of the Government Center Facilities Operation and Maintenance Agreement between the City and the Cedar Hill Independent School District (School). The discussion included review of the timelines, the memorandum of understanding, concepts for the agreement, allocation formulas, and the administrative structure of the agreement.

City Manager Alan Sims asked for input from the City Council on the dispute resolution process. The City Council preferred a joint committee similar to the executive committee for the dispute resolution process.

The City Council provided direction regarding additional deal points to be considered in the agreement, including use of the architectural review committee and working out temporary buildings contractually.

The concepts discussed will be included in the draft Operation and Maintenance Agreement.

III. Adjourn.

There being no further business, Mayor Franke adjourned the meeting at 7:40 p.m.

_____

Rob Franke, Mayor

MINUTES — CITY COUNCIL SPECIAL MEETING

ATTEST:

_____

Frankie Lee, City Secretary

NOTICE OF SPECIAL MEETING

CITY COUNCIL

CITY OF CEDAR HILL

STRATEGIC PLANNING RETREAT

OCTOBER 19-20, 2007

WHITE BLUFF RESORT — LAKE WHITNEY

22 MISTY VALLEY CIRCLE

WHITNEY, TEXAS 76692

MISSION STATEMENT: The mission of the City of Cedar Hill is to deliver the highest quality municipal services to our citizens and customers, consistent with our community values.

VISION STATEMENT: We envision Cedar Hill as a premier city that retains its distinctive character, where families and businesses flourish in a safe and clean environment.

AGENDA

FRIDAY, OCTOBER 19, 2007

I. 11:30 a.m. — Arrival

II. 12:00 p.m. — Lunch (Trophy Grille)

III. 1:00 p.m. — (Conference Center, Room C)

a. Call the meeting to order.

b. Conduct a visioning and goal-setting work session.

IV. 5:30 p.m. — Recess

NOTICE OF SPECIAL MEETING

V. 6:00 p.m. — Dinner (Lighthouse Restaurant)

VI. 7:30 p.m. — (Conference Center, Room C)

Reconvene and continue visioning and goal-setting work session.

VII. Adjourn for the day.

SATURDAY, OCTOBER 20, 2007

I. 8:00 a.m. — Breakfast (Trophy Grille)

II. 9:00 a.m. — (Conference Center, Room C)

a. Call the meeting to order.

b. Continue visioning and goal-setting work session.

III. 12:00 p.m. — Lunch (Trophy Grille)

IV. 1:00 p.m. (Conference Center, Room C)

Continue visioning and goal-setting work session.

V. Adjourn.

DRIVING DIRECTIONS TO WHITE BLUFF RESORT:

From Dallas/Ft. Worth:

Take I-35 South and take Exit 370 (Spur 579) west to Hillsboro. At the "Old Courthouse" in Hillsboro, take a right going west on Highway 22 to Whitney (11 miles). Take the right fork at the Exxon Station (Loop 180) in Whitney and continue to the traffic light. Turn right at the traffic light onto Highway 933. White Bluff Resort is approximately 6 miles on the left.

I certify that the above notice of meeting was posted in accordance with the Texas Open Meetings Act on the 15th day of October 2007.

NOTICE OF SPECIAL MEETING

Frankie Lee

City Secretary

This facility is wheelchair accessible. Handicap parking spaces are available. To make arrangements for sign interpretative services or special accommodations, please call 972-291-5100 Ext. 1011 or (TDD) 1-800-RELAY TX (1-800-735-2989) at least 48 hours ahead of the meeting.

PREMIER STATEMENTS

CEDAR HILL HAS EXCELLENT, SAFE & EFFICIENT MOBILITY

CEDAR HILL IS SAFE

CEDAR HILL IS CLEAN

CEDAR HILL HAS TEXAS SCHOOLS OF CHOICE

CEDAR HILL HAS VIBRANT PARKS AND NATURAL BEAUTY

CEDAR HILL HAS A STRONG AND DIVERSE ECONOMY

Appendix II
Sample Bylaws Structure

ARTICLES

Article I — This article states the name of the organization.

Article II — This article states the reason the organization is in existence. A general statement is made here as to what the organization will do and how it will function on a daily basis, who the group is and what it aspires to in order to stay alive.

Article III — This article lists information about membership. There are many different member options and levels, and therefore this should be thought through clearly to involve everyone without making it too open if that is not the purpose.

Section One might address the different levels of membership, from student membership to general membership to executive level-members.

Section Two will address the fees or dues that each member at each level must pay to be a part of the organization.

Section Three addresses how a person can join the group. What are the eligibility requirements for membership, and how is this done? Will membership be on a yearly basis or in the month that the person joins?

Section Four allows for the members to know what rights they have once they join the group. In some cases student members might not be able to vote, or associate members might be in name only and not have voting privileges. All these items need to be addressed.

Section Five covers how a person may resign from a position. Is there a time limit, or can a person just quit on a whim?

ARTICLES

Section Six will address how to handle problems and the disciplining of members and/or officers if needed.

Article IV — This article will address the officers who need to be voted into the various positions of the organization and what these positions might be, such as a president, vice president, secretary, and treasurer. Sometimes a vice president might also be the treasurer. Another point to note is there might be more than one vice president. Perhaps there is a vice president of benefits, a vice president of computers, and a vice president at large. You can also list other director positions here as well. In an entertainment organization you might have, for example, director of professional development, director of membership, director of programs, and director of communications.

Section One will list the names of the officers and the order of rank that each person will have in the organization. This will help if there is a question as to who is in charge when the president or presiding officer is out.

Section Two will list the duties of each person in each position so there is no question as to what is expected and what is overstepping the line in each particular position.

Section Three will detail how long each position will stay in office. These times can also be staggered so an entire organization does not have turnover at one time.

Section Four explains how each officer will be nominated and put into the given position.

Article V — This article will deal with the meetings and how they are to be conducted as well as how often.

Section One discusses the regular meeting and when it will take place. Many companies and organizations have monthly meetings open to the membership.

Section Two will highlight the particulars of the yearly meeting and what members need to know about this meeting.

Section Three details how special meetings are to be called and for the various reasons they can and cannot be called.

Section Four gives the number of voting members that must be present in order for a quorum to be considered and a meeting to be legal.

ARTICLES

Article VI — Committees are addressed here: if there will be any committees and how these committees will be formed and function. Not all committees will be mentioned in the bylaws and can be appointed as special committees. However, committees that will have a place in the organization on an ongoing basis should be named here as well as how many members the committee must have the duties of the committee members and how these members will be chosen.

Article VII relates to how the meetings will be held (this is where Robert's Rules come in handy). The article can go into detail with each rule and how motions are to be carried out or note perhaps that meetings will be conducted based on, for example, Robert's Rules.

Article VIII — This article notes how the bylaws can be amended. Normally, amending bylaws entails letting all the members know in advance that this is going to happen as well as when and where. Also noted will be if the amendment needs a majority vote or a two-thirds vote.

Article IX — This article, or whatever article is the last in the bylaws, discusses how to dissolve an organization. This is required by the IRS for tax purposes. What is known as a dissolution clause will explain in detail how the organization is to be disbanded legally. For organizations that are also incorporated, this information might be found within those documents as well.

Appendix III
Sample Committee Report

REPORT OF THE CITY OF XYZ

Special Committee on Going Green

April 30, 20XX

The committee contacted 10 cities in the surrounding area during the time from January to March of 20XX. The committee was seeking information on how many cities in the surrounding area had gone green and what means they had used to do this for their citizens.

In the first meeting the committee discussed the various surrounding cities and determined the 10 that most easily met the same populations and patterns as XYZ. The following cities were chosen:

City 1

City 2

City 3

City 4

City 5

City 6

City 7

City 8

City 9

City 10

REPORT OF THE CITY OF XYZ

One committee spokesperson spoke with the City Manager of each city and asked the following questions:

How long has your city been "green?"

What benefits have you found in going green?

What challenges have you found in maintaining a green status?

What are some of the ways you have incorporated these green areas into the community?

How much money have you saved or lost on going green?

What are the lasting benefits of this change to your city?

The Special Committee on Going Green has found that there are many good reasons for going green in the long and short run. Only two out of the 10 cities lost money going green, and most reported that the challenges were minimal. City officials have found that residents are eager to be a part of the bigger solution of helping to save the environment, and with this they are more apt to recycle, throw trash in available bins, and use lower-watt light bulbs when given the incentive to do so. The lasting benefits to these changes include the city's ability to feel good about saving the environment, and one city started a "plant a new tree every week" program as well.

The Special Committee on Going Green's recommendations are that City XYZ also implement a going green plan for residents citywide and give them option of things they can do to save the environment with help from the city.

Molly Green, Chairman

Special Committee on Going Green

Appendix IV
Sample Resolution

SAMPLE RESOLUTION

RESOLUTION NO.

WHEREAS, the City Council of XYZ believes it to be in the best interest of the citizens of XYZ to enter into a joint election agreement with other entities in ABC County holding elections on May 10, 2008, to be administered by the ABC Elections Department,

NOW, THEREFORE, BE it resolved by the City Council of the City of XYZ, that:

SECTION 1. The City of XYZ shall enter into a joint election agreement and election service contract for the conduct of the General Election to be held on Saturday, May 10, 2008, in the City of XYZ, to be administered by the ABC County Elections Department.

SECTION 2. The City Secretary is hereby authorized to negotiate the final details of the election with the ABC County Elections Department and approve any amendments to the agreement and election service contract.

SECTION 3. The ABC County Elections Administrator is hereby instructed to notify the election judges serving at each polling place where voters of the City of XYZ participate to release the unofficial election results to the City Secretary of the City of XYZ, or her designee, from each polling place shortly after the close of the voting.

SECTION 4. Mayor (insert name) is hereby authorized to execute the joint agreement and election services contract authorized herein.

SAMPLE RESOLUTION

SECTION 5.   This Resolution shall be attached to the joint election agreement and election services contract authorized herein.

PASSED, ADOPTED AND APPROVED by the City Council of the City of XYZ on this 26th day of February, 2008.

_____

Mayor

ATTEST:

_____

City Secretary

Appendix V
Sample Ordinance

SAMPLE ORDINANCE

ORDINANCE NO.

AN ORDINANCE OF THE CITY OF XYZ, PROVIDING FOR A STREET NAME OF A CITY STREET AS DESCRIBED HEREIN AND PROVIDING AN EFFECTIVE DATE.

WHEREAS, the City Council of the City of XYZ has determined that it is in the best interest of the City and general public to name streets within the City of XYZ in a manner that does not cause confusion to emergency services and the general public; and

WHEREAS, a new connector road has been constructed between No Name Boulevard and Unknown Road; and

WHEREAS, the City Council has reached out to the community to determine a favorable name for the street named herein,

NOW, THEREFORE, BE IT ORDAINED by the City Council of the City of XYZ that:

Section 1. Naming of Street

A connector street constructed between No Name Boulevard and Unknown Road, shown on Exhibit A attached hereto, is hereby named "Brand New Trail."

Section 2. Effective Date

The ordinance shall become effective and be in full force and effect from and after the date of passage and publication as required by law.

PASSED, APPROVED AND ADOPTED by the City Council of the City of XYZ on this 26th day of February 2008.

SAMPLE ORDINANCE

APPROVED

_____
Mayor

ATTEST:

_____

City Secretary

APPROVED AS TO FORM

_____

City Attorney

Appendix VI

Conventions

Not all organizations will find it necessary to hold a convention or assembly of delegates. But when this is the case, Robert's Rules of Order are specific about what this is and how it is to be handled. The following is taken from the 4th Edition of Robert's Rules of Order:

Meeting of a Convention or Assembly of Delegates. *(a) An Organized Convention.* If a convention is an organized body (that is, if when convened it has a constitution and by-laws and officers), a committee on credentials, or registration, and one on program, should have been appointed previous to the meeting. These committees may have been appointed at the previous convention, or by the executive board, or by the president, as prescribed by the by-laws. The committee on credentials, or registration, should be on hand somewhat before the time of the meeting, in some cases the day before, so as to be prepared to submit its report immediately after the opening addresses. It should furnish each delegate, when he registers, with a badge or card as evidence of his being a delegate and having the right of admission to the hall. The committee on program should in most cases have the programs printed in advance. In many cases it is better that the constituent bodies be furnished in advance with copies of the program. This should always be done when there is difficulty in getting full delegations to attend. In addition to these two committees there are a number of local committees usually appointed by the local society, as on entertainment, etc. One of the general officers usually performs the duty of a committee on transportation, to obtain reductions in railroad fares, etc.

When the hour appointed for the meeting arrives, the president, as the permanent presiding officer of a convention is usually called, stands at the desk, and, striking it with the gavel to attract attention, says, "The convention will come to order." In large conventions there is usually much confusion and noise at the opening, and it requires self-control, firmness, and tact on the part of the presiding officer to preserve proper order so that all members may hear and be heard. It is a mistake for the chairman to try to stop the noise by pounding with the gavel and talking so loud as to be heard in spite of conversation on the floor. It is better for him to set the example of being quiet, and to stop all business while the noise is such that members cannot hear. Members should be required to be seated and to refrain from talking except when addressing the chair.

When the convention has come to order it is customary to have some opening exercises, the nature of which depends upon the character of the convention. In the majority of cases the convention is opened with prayer, an address of welcome, and a response. The program, however, is the president's guide as to the order of business, even though it has not yet been adopted by the convention. It should provide for hearing the report of the credential committee as soon as the opening exercises are concluded, so that it may be known who are entitled to vote. This committee's report usually consists merely of a list of the delegates and their alternates, if any, whose credentials have been found correct, and of the ex officio members of the convention, no one being on the list, however, who has not registered as present. The constitution should always provide that such as are present of the officers of the convention, the members of the Board of Managers, and the chairmen of the committees that are required to report at the convention, shall be ex officio members of the convention.

When this report of the credential committee is presented it is read either by the chairman of the committee or by the reading secretary, or official reader, if there is one. In all cases, it, and all other reports, should be read from the platform. When the chairman of a committee cannot read so as to be heard, the report should be read by a reading secretary, or official reader, who should be appointed in every large convention, solely for the purpose of reading resolutions, reports, etc. If there is a case of contest between two sets of delegates and there is serious doubt as to which is entitled to recognition, the committee should omit both from the list and report the fact of the contest. If the committee, however, thinks the contest not justified, it should ignore it and enter on the list the names of the legitimate delegates. A motion should be made to accept or adopt the report, which, after it is stated by the chair, is open to debate and amendment. No one can vote whose name is not on the list of delegates reported by the committee. Upon the motion to substitute one delegation for another, neither one can vote. So upon a motion to strike out the names of a delegation whose seats are contested they cannot vote. But upon the main motion to accept the report, all persons whose names are on the list of members as reported by the committee and amended by the convention are entitled to vote, and they alone. When this report has been adopted, the president should immediately call upon the program committee for a report. The chairman of that committee submits the printed program and moves, or some one else moves, its adoption. This is open to debate and amendment, and when once adopted by a majority vote can not be deviated from except by a two-thirds vote of those voting, or by a majority vote of the enrolled membership.

The membership of the convention and the program having been decided, the convention is ready for its business as laid down in the program. The two committees, though they have made their reports, are continued through the session, as supplementary reports may be required from them. Additional delegates may arrive, and speakers on the program may be sick or unable to be present, or for other reasons a change in the program may be necessary. These two committees should be allowed at any time to make additional reports. The business is conducted as described in the preceding section, but, of course, the program must be followed. Boards and standing committees and the treasurer are always required to submit annual reports, and sometimes reports are required from various other officers. Generally officers and the board of managers, etc., are elected annually; but some constitutions make the term of office two years, and some provide, in addition, that only about half the officers shall be elected at any one annual meeting. In most organizations it is better to have the term of office begin at the close of the convention, so that the same officers will serve throughout the meetings. At the beginning of the first meeting each day the minutes of the preceding day are read and approved. At the close of the convention, if there is not time to read the minutes of the last day, a motion should be adopted authorizing the board, or some committee, to approve the minutes of that day. As the proceedings of a convention are usually published, a publishing committee should be appointed, which should have the power to edit the proceedings. When through with its business the convention adjourns sine die.

(b) *A Convention not yet Organized.* Such a convention is similar to a mass meeting, already described in 69, in that when called to order it has no constitution, by-laws, or officers. It has the added difficulty of determining who are entitled to vote. In the mass meeting every one may vote, but in the convention none but properly appointed delegates may vote, and sometimes this is a very difficult question to determine justly. The convention must have been called by some committee, or body of men, who should have secured the hall and made the preliminary arrangements for the meeting. If the convention is a very large one, so that it is necessary to reserve the main floor of the hall for the delegates, the committee should allow only those to enter who have prima facie evidence of their right to membership, and in contested cases both sides should be admitted. The chairman of the committee should call the convention to order, and either he or some one the committee has selected for the purpose should nominate a temporary chairman and a temporary secretary. Next should come the appointment of a committee on credentials, whose duty it is to examine all credentials and report a list of all the delegates who are entitled to seats in the convention. When alternates have been appointed they should be reported also. While the committee on credentials is out, committees may be appointed on nominations of officers, on rules, and on order of business or program. In a large convention of this kind all committees should be appointed by the chair, and no one whose right to a seat is questioned should be placed on a committee until the convention has acted favorably on his case. Until the committee on credentials has reported, no business can be done except to authorize the chair to appoint the above mentioned committees. While waiting for the committee on credentials to report, the time is usually spent in listening to speeches. When the committee reports, the procedure is the same as just described in an organized convention. When that report has been adopted, the convention proceeds to its permanent organization, acting upon the reports of the other three committees previously appointed, taking them in such order as the convention pleases. When these reports have been acted upon, the convention is organized, with members, officers, rules, and program, and its business is transacted as in other organized deliberative assemblies. If the convention adopts rules only for the session, the committee on rules need recommend only a few rules as to the hours for beginning the meetings, the length of the speeches, etc., and a rule adopting some standard rules of order, where not in conflict with its other rules. If it is not intended to make a permanent organization, the organization just described is all that is necessary.

If the convention is called to make a permanent organization, the committee on nominations is not appointed until after the by-laws are adopted, and the committee on rules should report a constitution and by-laws as in the case of a permanent society [70]. The committee in such case is more usually called the committee on constitution and by-laws. When a convention of this kind is composed of delegates away from their homes it is practically impossible to have them assemble more frequently than once a year, and, therefore, before the convention meets, a constitution and by-laws should be carefully drafted by those interested in calling the convention. Those who drew up the by-laws should be appointed on the committee, in order to avoid delay in reporting them.

After the committee has reported a constitution and by-laws the procedure is the same as already described in the previous section in case of acting on a constitution and by-laws for a permanent society [70(b)]. When the by-laws are adopted, the officers are elected and committees are appointed as prescribed by the by-laws, and the convention is prepared for its work as already described.

❧Appendix VII

Using Robert's Rules as a Roadmap

Although there are many editions of Robert's Rules of Order since the first copy was written and used by the original author, the main reason for writing the document and keeping meetings in order has not changed. Below is the introduction to the fourth edition of Robert's Rules of Order. This is an excellent tool for understanding the changes that have taken place since the fourth edition and how much many of the similarities still remain. It will also give you a good idea of where to begin when creating your own rules for your organization as in what to change and what to keep regarding Robert's Rules of Order.

Introduction

Parliamentary Law

Parliamentary Law refers originally to the customs and rules for conducting business in the English Parliament; and thence to the usages of deliberative assemblies in general. In England these usages of Parliament form a part of the unwritten law of the land, and in our own legislative bodies they are of authority in all cases where they do not conflict with existing rules or precedents.

But as a people we have not the respect which the English have for customs and precedents, and are always ready for such innovations as we think are improvements; hence changes have been and are constantly being made in the written rules which our legislative bodies have found best to adopt. As each house adopts its own rules, the result is that the two houses of the same legislature do not always agree in their practice; even in Congress the order of precedence of motions is not the same in both houses, and the previous question is admitted in the House of Representatives but not in the Senate. As a consequence of this, the exact method of conducting business in any particular legislative body is to be obtained only from the Legislative Manual of that body.

The vast number of societies — political, literary, scientific, benevolent, and religious — formed all over the land, though not legislative, are deliberative in character, and must have some system of conducting business and some rules to govern their proceedings, and are necessarily subject to the common parliamentary law where it does not conflict with their own special rules. But as their knowledge of parliamentary law has been obtained from the usages in this country, rather than from the customs of Parliament, it has resulted that these societies have followed in part the customs of our own legislative bodies, and our people have thus been educated under a system of parliamentary law which is peculiar to this country, and yet so well established as to supersede the English parliamentary law as the common law of ordinary deliberative assemblies.

The practice of the National House of Representatives should have the same force in this country as the usages of the House of Commons have in England, in determining the general principles of the common parliamentary law of the land, were it not for the fact that while the English Parliament has continued to be a strictly deliberative assembly, the business of our House of Representatives has grown so enormously that it has been obliged to make such changes in its rules and practice as will allow the majority to suppress the debate, if there has been previous debate, and if there has been none, to limit the debate to forty minutes; and also to suppress a question for the session even without any debate. These deviations from the old parliamentary law, while necessary in the House of Representatives, are in violation of the fundamental right of a deliberative assembly to have questions thoroughly discussed before it is called upon to take action upon them, unless a large majority, at least two-thirds, is prepared to act at once. In ordinary deliberative assemblies the right to debate questions before taking final action upon them should never be suppressed by less than a two-thirds vote, and the motion to lay on the table should be used only for its legitimate parliamentary purpose of laying aside a question temporarily.

Where the practice of Congress differs from that of Parliament, the common law of this country usually follows the practice of Congress. Thus, in every American deliberative assembly having no rules for conducting business, the motion to adjourn, when it does not dissolve the assembly, would be decided to be undebatable, as in Congress, the English parliamentary law to the contrary notwithstanding; so if the previous question were negative, the debate upon the subject would continue, as in Congress, whereas in Parliament the subject would be immediately dismissed; so, too, the previous question could be moved when there was before the assembly a motion either to commit, or to postpone definitely or indefinitely, just as in Congress, notwithstanding that, according to English parliamentary law, the previous question could not be moved under such circumstances.

The old common parliamentary law gives the same rank to the motions for the previous question, to postpone definitely, to commit, and to postpone indefinitely, so that no one of them can be moved while another one of them is pending; the House makes them rank in the order just named; while the Senate does not admit the motion for the previous question, and makes to postpone indefinitely outrank all the others. The practice of the House in this matter establishes the parliamentary law of this country, as it does in all cases where its practice is not due to the great quantity of its business or the necessities of party government. This may be illustrated by the motions to lay on the table and the previous question. The House of Representatives has completely changed the use of the motion to lay on the table from that of merely laying aside a question until the assembly chooses to resume its consideration [see foot note, 28], to a motion to kill the pending proposition. To make it more effective for this purpose, they have allowed it to be made before the member reporting a bill from the committee is allowed to speak, and when a question is laid upon the table it cannot be taken up except by suspending the rules, which requires a two-thirds vote. For reasons previously given, such rules are necessary in Congress, but in ordinary assemblies they would do more harm than good. The same vote should be required (two-thirds vote) to stop debate and bring the assembly to a vote on the final disposition of the question, whether the intention is to adopt or to reject the proposition. The previous question and the motion to lay on the table require the same vote in Congress, and should in all assemblies where to lay on the table is used for killing propositions.

The modifications made by the House in regard to the previous question have made that motion extremely simple and useful, and its practice establishes the parliamentary law of the country as to the previous question, except in respect to its being ordered by majority vote and forty minutes' debate being allowed after it has been ordered, if the proposition has no been previously debated. It is necessary in Congress for the majority to have the power to close debate, but, such a power being in conflict with the fundamental rights of a deliberative assembly, Congress has modified it so as not to cut off debate entirely. In an ordinary assembly, with sessions not exceeding two or three hours, it should, and it does, have the power by a two-thirds vote to close debate instantly, just as by the same vote it may suspend the rules.

In matters of detail, the rules of the House of Representatives are adapted to the peculiar wants of that body, and are of no authority in any other assembly. No one, for instance, would accept the following House of Representatives rules as common parliamentary law in this country: That the chairman, in case of disorderly conduct, would have the power to order the galleries to be cleared; that any fifteen members would be authorized to compel the attendance of absent members; that each member would be limited in debate upon any question to one hour; and that the motion to suspend the rules can only be entertained on the first and third Mondays of each month. These examples are sufficient to show the absurdity of the idea that the rules of Congress in all things determine the common parliamentary law.

While some of the rules of Congress are adapted only to legislative assemblies, and others only to the House that adopts them, yet its rules and practice, except where manifestly unsuited to ordinary deliberative assemblies, should, and do determine the parliamentary law of the country. The people of the United States will never accept the rules and practice of the legislature, or of deliberative assemblies, of any state, or even of any section of the country, as of equal authority with the practice of the National Congress in determining the parliamentary law for the whole country.

Since, however, the sessions of Congress last from three to six months, and at times to nearly a year, whereas the great majority of ordinary deliberative assemblies have sessions lasting not more than two or three hours; and since the quorum in Congress is a majority of the members, while in most societies it is less than one-fifth, and often less than one-tenth, of the members; and since the members of Congress are paid to devote all their time during a session to the business of Congress, and can be compelled to attend, whereas in ordinary assemblies the members have other duties and their attendance is simply voluntary; and as the work of Congress is enormous and is mostly done by standing committees, of which there are fifty-six, or in committee of the whole, while in ordinary assemblies the assembly itself attends to most of its business, the rest is done usually by special committees rather than by standing committees or in committee of the whole — as these differences exist, it is evident that the rules and practice of Congress require to be modified in some respects to adapt them to ordinary deliberative assemblies. Sometimes the old common parliamentary law is better adapted to ordinary societies, as with the motion to lay on the table. Where the two houses differ, sometimes the Senate practice is better adapted to ordinary assemblies, as in allowing each member to speak twice to the same question each day; while in allowing the previous question and in making the motion to postpone indefinitely the lowest of subsidiary motions, the practice of the House seems better adapted to ordinary assemblies. The House allows a majority to order the previous question, but if there has been no debate on the question, forty minutes' debate is permitted after the previous question has been ordered. This rule is not adapted to assemblies whose entire session may not last two hours. They should have power to close debate instantly by a two-thirds vote. This is in accordance with the general principle that the assembly by a two-thirds vote may suspend the rules, even the rule permitting debate.

As there would naturally be differences of opinion as to the application of the above principles, and it is important that the law should be definite, every deliberative assembly should imitate our legislative bodies and adopt some Rules of Order for the conduct of its business.

Plan of the Work

These Rules are prepared to meet partially this want in deliberative assemblies that are not legislative in their character. They have been made sufficiently complete to answer for the rules of an assembly until it sees fit to adopt special rules conflicting with and superseding any of the rules of detail, such as the Order of Business, etc. They are based upon the rules and practice of Congress so far as these are adapted to ordinary deliberative assemblies with short sessions and comparatively small quorums, as has just been explained. In cases where these Rules differ from the practice of Congress, usually the congressional rule will be found in a foot note. The foot notes need not be referred to for any other purpose than to ascertain the practice of Congress.

This Manual contains a Table of Contents, Table of Rules, Part I, Part II, Lesson Outlines, and the Index.

Table of Contents. This gives a clear, systematic idea of the arrangement of subjects treated in the Manual.

Order of Precedence of Motions and Table of Rules. A careful study of these tables so as to be able to use them quickly will enable any one in an emergency to ascertain whether a motion is in order, and whether it may be debated, or amended, or reconsidered, or requires a second, or a two-thirds vote, or is in order when another member has the floor.

Part I, comprising the main part of the Manual, contains a set of Rules of Order systematically arranged, as shown in the Table of Contents. It begins with showing how business is introduced in a deliberative assembly, and then follows it step by step until the vote is taken and announced. The next section, 10, shows what is the proper motion to use to accomplish certain objects, referring at the same time to the section where the motion will be found fully treated. Next, the motions are classified as usual into Privileged, Incidental, Subsidiary, and Main, and the general characteristics of each class given.

Then each class is taken up in order, beginning with the highest privileged motion, and a section is devoted to each motion, including some motions that are not classified. Each of these 26 sections is complete in itself, so that one unfamiliar with the work need not be misled in examining any particular subject. Cross-references, in heavy-face type, are used wherever it was thought they would be helpful, the references being to sections, the number of the section being placed at the top of each page. The following is stated in reference to each motion, except some of the incidental ones, the first six points being mentioned at the beginning of each section:

(1) Of what motions it *takes precedence* (that is, what motions may be pending and yet it be in order to make and consider this motion).

(2) To what motions it *yields* (that is, what motions may be made and considered while this motion is pending).

(3) Whether it is *debatable* or not (all motions being debatable unless the contrary is stated).

(4) Whether it can be *amended* or not.

(5) In case the motion can have no subsidiary motion *applied* to it, the fact is stated [see **Adjourn**, 17, for an example: the meaning is, that the particular motion, to adjourn, cannot be laid on the table, postponed, committed, or amended, etc.].

(6) The *vote* required for its adoption, when it is not a majority.

(7) The *form* of making the motion when peculiar.

(8) The *form of stating and putting the question* when peculiar.

(9) The *object* of the motion when not apparent.

(10) The *effect* of the motion if adopted, whenever it could possibly be misunderstood.

Part II contains an explanation of the methods of organizing and conducting different kinds of meetings, giving the words used by the chairman and speakers in making and putting various motions; and also a few pages devoted to the legal rights of deliberative assemblies and ecclesiastical tribunals, and to the trial of members of such societies. The beginner especially, will find it useful to read sections 69-71 in connection with sections 1-10, thus obtaining correct ideas as to the methods of conducting business in deliberative assemblies.

The Plan for the Study of Parliamentary Law gives some helpful suggestions to clubs and individuals wishing to study parliamentary law together with a series of eighteen Lesson Outlines.

The Index refers to pages, not sections, and at the beginning are given some suggestions as to the best method of finding anything in these Rules.

Definitions

In addition to the terms defined above (*taking precedence of, yielding to, and applying to* [see above]), there are other terms that are liable to be misunderstood, to which attention is called.

Accepting a report is the same as adopting it, and must be decided before the pending question, should not be confused with *receiving* a report, which is allowing it to be presented to the assembly.

Assembly. This term is used for the deliberative assembly, and should be replaced in motions, etc., by the proper name of the body, as society, club, church, board, convention, etc.

The *Chair* means the presiding officer, whether temporary or permanent.

The terms *Congress* and *H.R.*, when used in this Manual, refer to the U.S. House of Representatives.

Meeting and *Session*. Meeting is used in this Manual for an assembling of the members of a deliberative body for any length of time during which they do not separate for longer than a few minutes, as the morning meeting, or the evening meeting, of a convention. In a society with rules providing for regular meetings every week, or month, etc., each of these regular meetings is a separate session. A called or special meeting is a distinct session. Should a regular or special meeting adjourn to meet at another time, the adjourned meeting is a continuation of the session, not a separate one; the two meetings constitute one session. In the case of a convention holding a meeting every year or two, or rather a series of meetings lasting several days, the entire series of meetings constitute one session. [See 63.]

Pending and *Immediately Pending*. A question is said to be pending when it has been stated by the chair and has not yet disposed of either permanently or temporarily. When several questions are pending, the one last stated by the chair, and therefore the one to be first disposed of, is said to be the immediately pending question.

A *Main motion* is one that is made to bring before the assembly any particular subject. No main motion can be made when another motion is pending.

A *Subsidiary* motion is one that may be applied to a main motion, and to certain other motions, for the purpose of modifying them, delaying action upon them or otherwise disposing of them.

Privileged motions are such that, although having no relation to the pending question, are of such urgency or importance as to require them to take precedence of all other motions.

An *Incidental motion* is one that arises out of another question which is pending or has just been pending, and must be decided before the pending question, or before other business is taken up. Incidental motions have no fixed rank but take precedence of the questions out of which they arise, whether those questions are main or subsidiary or privileged.

The *Previous Question* docs not refer, as its name would imply, to the previous question, but is the name given to the motion to close debate and at once to take the vote on the immediately pending question and such other questions as are specified in the motion.

A *Substitute* is an amendment where an entire resolution, or section, or one or more paragraphs, is struck out and another resolution, or section, or one or more paragraphs, is inserted in its place.

Plurality, *Majority*, and *Two-thirds Vote*. In an election a candidate has a plurality when he has a larger vote than any other candidate; he has a majority when he has more than half the votes cast, ignoring blanks. In an assembly a plurality never elects except by virtue of a rule to that effect. A majority vote when used in these rules means a majority of the votes cast, ignoring blanks, at a legal meeting, a quorum being present. A two-thirds vote is two-thirds of the votes just described. For an illustration of the difference between a two-thirds vote, a vote of two-thirds of the members present, and a vote of two-thirds of the members.

Appendix VIII

Motions

As mentioned in the body of this book, motions are one of the most important items relating to Robert's Rules of Order and how meetings are run correctly. With just the various motions, rules are adopted and challenges are brought up and handled in the spirit of proper meeting procedures. Below is a list from the fourth edition of Robert's Rules of Order of the motions and the definitions that were stated when the original book was written.

ART. II. GENERAL CLASSIFICATION OF MOTIONS	
For convenience motions may be classified as follows:	
Main or Principal Motions	11
Subsidiary Motions	12
Incidental Motions	13
Privileged Motions	14

11. A Main or Principal Motion is a motion made to bring before the assembly, for its consideration, any particular subject. It takes precedence of nothing — that is, it cannot be made when any other question is before the assembly; and it yields to all Privileged, Incidental, and Subsidiary Motions — that is, any of these motions can be made while a main motion is pending. Main motions are debatable, and subject to amendment, and can have any subsidiary [12] motions applied to them. When a main motion is laid on the table, or postponed to a certain time, it carries with it all pending subsidiary motions. If a main motion is referred to a committee it carries with it only the pending amendments. As a general rule, they require for their adoption only a majority vote — that is, a majority of the votes cast; but amendments to constitutions, by-laws, and rules of order already adopted, all of which are main motions, require a two-thirds vote for their adoption, unless the by-laws, etc., specify a different vote for their amendment; and the motion to rescind action previously taken requires a two-thirds vote, or a vote of a majority of the entire membership, unless previous notice of the motion has been given.

Main motions may be subdivided into *Original Main Motions* and *Incidental Main Motions*. Original Main Motions are those which bring before the assembly some new subject, generally in the form of a resolution, upon which action by the assembly is desired. Incidental Main Motions are those main motions that are incidental to, or relate to, the business of the assembly, or its past or future action, as, a committee's report on a resolution referred to it. A motion to accept or adopt the report of a standing committee upon a subject not referred to it is an original main motion, but a motion to adopt a report on a subject referred to a committee is an incidental main motion. The introduction of an original main motion can be prevented by sustaining by a two-thirds vote an objection to its consideration [23], made just after the main motion is stated and before it is discussed. An objection to its consideration cannot be applied to an incidental main motion, but a two-thirds vote can immediately suppress it by ordering the previous question [29]. This is the only difference between the two classes of main motions. The following list contains some of the most common Incidental Main Motions.

COMMON INCIDENTAL MAIN MOTIONS	
Accept or Adopt a report upon a subject referred to a committee	54
Adjourn at, or to, a future time	17
Adjourn, if qualified in any way, or to adjourn when the effect is to dissolve the assembly with no provision for its reconvening	17
Appoint the Time and Place for the next meeting, if introduced when no business is pending	16
Amend the Constitution, By-laws, Standing Rules, or Resolutions, etc., already adopted	68
Ratify or Confirm action taken	39
Rescind or Repeal action taken	37

All of these motions are essentially main motions and are treated as such, though they may appear otherwise.

Though a question of privilege is of high rank so far as interrupting a pending question is concerned, yet when the question has interrupted business and is pending, it is treated as a main motion so far as having incidental and subsidiary motions applied to it. So an order of the day, even though a special order, after it has been taken up is treated in the same way, as is also a question that has been reconsidered.

No motion is in order that conflicts with the constitution, by-laws, or standing rules or resolutions of the assembly, and if such a motion is adopted it is null and void. Before introducing such a motion it is necessary to amend the constitution or by-laws, or amend or rescind the conflicting standing rule or resolution. So, too, a motion is not in order that conflicts with a resolution previously adopted by the assembly at the same session, or that has been introduced and has not been finally disposed of. If it is not too late the proper course is to reconsider [36] the vote on the motion previously adopted, and then amend it so as to express the desired idea. If it cannot be reconsidered, then by a two-thirds vote the old resolution may be rescinded when the new one can be introduced, or by giving notice it may be rescinded by a majority vote at the next meeting. In ordinary societies, where the quorum is a small percentage of the membership, and the meetings are as frequent as quarterly, no resolution that conflicts with one adopted at a previous session should be entertained until the old one has been rescinded, which requires a two-thirds vote unless proper notice has been given.

12. Subsidiary Motions are such as are applied to other motions for the purpose of most appropriately disposing of them. By means of them the original motion may be modified, or action postponed, or it may be referred to a committee to investigate and report, etc. They may be applied to any main motion, and when made they supersede the main motion and must be decided before the main motion can be acted upon. None of them, except the motion to amend and those that close or limit or extend the limits of debate, can be applied to a subsidiary, incidental (except an appeal in certain cases), or privileged motion. Subsidiary motions, except to lay on the table, the previous question, and postpone indefinitely, may be amended. The motions affecting the limits of debate may be applied to any debatable question regardless of its privilege, and require a two-thirds vote for their adoption. All those of lower rank than those affecting the limits of debate are debatable, the rest are not. The motion to amend anything that has already been adopted, as by-laws or minutes, is not a subsidiary motion but is a main motion and can be laid on the table or have applied to it any other subsidiary motion without affecting the by-laws or minutes, because the latter are not pending.

In the following list the subsidiary motions are arranged in the order of their precedence, the first one having the highest rank. When one of them is the immediately pending question every motion above it is in order, and every one below it is out of order. They are as follows:

SUBSIDIARY MOTIONS	
Lay on the Table	28
The Previous Question	29
Limit or Extend Limits of Debate	30
Postpone Definitely, or to a Certain Time	31
Commit or Refer, or Recommit	32
Amend	33
Postpone Indefinitely	34

13. Incidental Motions are such as arise out of another question which is pending, and therefore take precedence of and must be decided before the question out of which they rise; or, they are incidental to a question that has just been pending and should be decided before any other business is taken up. They yield to privileged motions, and generally to the motion to lay on the table. They are undebatable, except an appeal under certain circumstances as shown in 21. They cannot be amended except where they relate to the division of a question, or to the method of considering a question, or to methods of voting, or to the time when nominations or the polls shall be closed. No subsidiary motion, except to amend, can be applied to any of them except a debatable appeal. Whenever it is stated that all incidental motions take precedence of a certain motion, the incidental motions referred to are only those that are legitimately incidental at the time they are made. Thus, incidental motions take precedence of subsidiary motions, but the incidental motion to object to the consideration of a question cannot be made while a subsidiary motion is pending, as the objection is only legitimate against an original main motion just after it is stated, before it has been debated or there has been any subsidiary motion stated. The following list comprises most of those that may arise:

INCIDENTAL MOTIONS	
Questions of Order and Appeal	21
Suspension of the Rules	22
Objection to the Consideration of a Question	23
Division of a Question, and Consideration by Paragraph or Seriatim	24
Division of the Assembly, and Motions relating to Methods of Voting, or to Closing or to Reopening the Polls	25
Motions relating to Methods of Making, or to Closing or to Reopening Nominations	26
Requests growing out of Business Pending or that has just been pending; as, a Parliamentary Inquiry, a Request for Information, for Leave to Withdraw a Motion, to Read Papers, to be Excused from a Duty, or for any other Privilege	27

14. Privileged Motions are such as, while not relating to the pending question, are of so great importance as to require them to take precedence of all other questions, and, on account of this high privilege, they are undebatable. They cannot have any subsidiary motion applied to them, except the motions to fix the time to which to adjourn, and to take a recess, which may be amended. But after the assembly has actually taken up the orders of the day or a question of privilege, debate and amendment are permitted and the subsidiary motions may be applied the same as on any main motion. These motions are as follows, being arranged in order of precedence:

PRIVILEGED MOTIONS	
Fix the Time to which to Adjourn (if made while another question is pending)	16
Adjourn (if unqualified and if it has not the effect to dissolve the assembly)	17
Take a Recess (if made when another question is pending)	18
Raise a Question of Privilege	19
Call for Orders of the Day	20

15. Some Main and Unclassified Motions. Two main motions (to rescind and to ratify) and several motions which cannot conveniently be classified as either Main, Subsidiary, Incidental, or Privileged, and which are in common use, are hereafter explained and their privileges and effects given. They are as follows:

SOME MAIN AND UNCLASSIFIED MOTIONS	
Take from the Table	35
Reconsider	36
Rescind	37
Renewal of a Motion	38
Ratify	39
Dilatory, Absurd, or Frivolous Motions	40
Call of the House	41

🌿Glossary

A

Absentee Voting: Voting for an item either through the mail or by a proxy vote. This must be noted as acceptable voting in the bylaws.

Abstain: To make the decision not to vote. When this happens, the person who decides not to vote is in consent regarding the decision made by the group who did vote.

Abstention: To abstain from a vote.

Accept: To adopt or approve a motion that has been put to a vote.

Acclamation: Undisputed consent.

Ad Hoc Committee: A special committee with the term meaning, in Latin, "to this."

Adhering Motions: Motions that are subsidiary, pending, and must be decided on before the main vote can be made.

Adjourn: Call the meeting to end by a motion.

Adjournment Sine Die: A Latin phrase that means

"without day." It is the final adjournment of a meeting or a convention, the last meeting of the meetings.

Adopt: To accept the motion.

Agenda: The list of predetermined items that will be discussed at the meeting, can also be called order of business.

Alternates: Substitute individuals taking the place of the person not able to attend the meeting.

Amend: To change a motion that is pending and perhaps change the motion before it is voted on by the group.

Amendment: A motion that changes an existing motion.

American Institute of Parliamentarians (AIP): A professional group of parliamentarians who understand and use Robert's Rules of Order on a regular basis as well as other parliamentary procedure.

Annual Meeting: This is a meeting that is held every year for the purpose of electing new officers and going over important yearly business.

Appeal: A motion to object to what the chair has ruled.

Appoint: To assign a person to sit on a committee or to take an office.

Assembly: A group of people in an organization who meet to talk about the decisions that will be made for the group as a whole.

Audit: A thorough exam of the financial records of an organization made by a committee, internal group, or sometimes the IRS.

B

Ballot vote: A vote that is not public, normally written on a piece of paper.

Board of Directors: A group of members who have been voted into this office to represent the organization and make decisions on the organization's behalf as necessary.

Budget: The amount of money to be spent in a given fiscal year, anticipated and actual.

Bylaws: The rules that are written for the running of a particular organization, the same as constitution.

C

Carried: To pass and adopt a motion.

Caucus: A meeting to determine how a particular motion will be addressed.

Censure: Letting the meeting know of official disapproval of what is happening in the meeting.

Chair/Chairman: The officer in charge of the meeting, can be the mayor, president, or CEO. Same as the presiding officer.

Charter: The Articles of Incorporation for an organization.

Chat Room: A form of electronic communication where people are logged in to the same online location and able to communicate in real time.

Circulated Agenda: The agenda for an upcoming meeting that has been passed to all the members who will participate in the meeting.

Close Nomination: To end the nominating process and hold the election. This cannot be done until all members have made the desired nominations.

Close the Polls: To end the accepting of ballots for the vote.

Commit: To send a pending motion to a group of members to study.

Committee: An appointed group of people chosen or elected to work on behalf of a particular issue in a number of ways, as determined by the group.

Committee Report: The findings of a committee, the official statement that is presented to the group in the name of the committee.

Conference Call: A telephone conversation in which members of the organization might be in different locations, but all can call in for a meeting on the telephone. All members can hear and discuss what is happening in the meeting.

Consent Agenda: A list of items on the meeting agenda that can be voted on in one vote without discussion on each.

These are fairly routine items, but items can be pulled for discussion and individual vote if requested.

Constitution: The rules of the organization and/or also called bylaws.

Convention: A meeting of delegates or members to make decisions for the organization.

Cumulative Voting: This is a type of voting that is done in order to fill open positions.

D

Debatable: A motion that is open for discussion from the members.

Debate: To discuss the motion in the meeting before voting.

Decorum: To act properly during the meeting.

Defer Action: Using a motion to postpone action on another motion.

Dilatory Motion: A motion that is irrelevant and unnecessary.

Discussion: The debate of an item or motion before the vote is taken by the members.

Division: To call for a recount of the existing vote.

Division of a Question: A motion that allows for voting on parts of a motion individually.

E

Electronic Meeting: Meetings that are held in more than one location by the use of telecommunication tools.

E-mail: A message that is sent electronically to another person from a computer or handheld device that is accessible as soon as a person retrieves it from an account, as opposed to instant messages, which appear on the screen as soon as they are sent.

Ex Officio: In Latin it means "by virtue of office." A member of the committee because of the office the person holds.

Executive Committee: A smaller part of the larger board or group that can make decisions if necessary between meetings, often composed of the officers of the organization.

Executive Session: A members-only meeting that is not open to the public.

F

Floor: Used in the term "to have the floor," which means to be the one in the position to speak.

Friendly Amendment: An amendment that the group agrees on without dissent.

G

Gavel: A mallet that the presiding officer uses to call a meeting to order and to adjourn a meeting.

General Consent: Unanimous agreement of the group.

General Order: A motion that was left pending in an earlier meeting.

Germane: Related to or having a direct influence on, pertaining to the subject.

I

Illegal Ballot: A ballot that for various reasons depending on the circumstance may not be counted as a vote.

In Order: The correct way of parliamentary procedure.

Incidental Motion: A motion relating to the procedural issues regarding various questions that might come up in the course of a motion being made.

Informal Consideration: A form of the committee as a group. This motion gives the members of the group a chance to offer ideas to each other within a framework that is more relaxing than the debate.

Item of Business: A report or a motion pertaining to a particular item in question.

L

Legal Vote: A vote that does count when cast at a meeting when a quorum is present for voting.

Limit Debate: To lessen the time that a person in the group may speak on an issue.

Lost Motion: A motion that did not win.

M

Main Motion: A motion that begins discussion of the group pertaining to a certain issue that will need to have an action taken on it.

Majority Vote: An additional one over half of the votes that are cast.

Meeting: A particular time when members gather to take care of the business of the organization

Member: A person who is a part of the organization through whatever means was necessary to join.

Minority: Any number of members that totals less than the number of members in attendance who are voting for a particular ruling. A minority vote would be four to three in the case where the three members voting were voting in the minority.

Minutes: The official written record of the meeting that was held.

Motion: The request that an action be taken regarding an item on the agenda that needs to have a vote set forth for approval or dismissal.

N

Negative Vote: A vote that goes against the existing motion that is being discussed and voted on.

New Business: Items that have not previously been brought before the organization for a vote.

Nomination: Naming a person as a candidate for an open position on the organization's board or group of elected officials.

Notice: An announcement in writing or given verbally of a motion that will be brought up at the meeting for discussion and a vote.

O

Officer: An elected official who holds office and adheres to the bylaws of the organization and is given certain duties to perform during the duration of office.

Old Business: A term that is no longer used and is often replaced by the term unfinished business, however it does have a separate meaning and is defined as business that has been completed.

On the Floor: A motion that is up for a vote after it has been stated clearly by the officer presiding over the meeting. The term pending also applies.

Order of Business: The schedule of the items that are being discussed and considered during the meeting.

Ordered: What has been voted on by the majority of the group and needs to be acted on.

Out of Order: When a person or group does not follow the proper parliamentary procedure.

P

Parliamentarian: A person who is well-versed in parliamentary procedure and might be hired by a group to give advice.

Parliamentary Authority: The manual that has been approved and adopted by the organization to serve as the governing power.

Parliamentary Inquiry: A question directed to the person in charge or presiding officer concerning parliamentary law and the group's personal rules.

Parliamentary Law/Procedure: The rules that have been set out by the organization's bylaws and that are used to keep order within a meeting as well as keeping the democratic process in place.

Pending: The motions and amendments that are to be discussed and voted on for action.

Pending Question: The motion that was last noted by the chair.

Plurality Vote: The option receiving the largest number of votes when there are more than two choices on the table.

Point of Information: A question that is not parliamentary but that does regard the business at hand.

Point of Order: An objection made by a member of the group for a procedure that was handled improperly.

Postpone Definitely: To change to a certain time in the future.

Postpone Indefinitely: This motion kills the main motion without a vote being needed.

Preamble: The introduction to a resolution that always begins with the wording "whereas."

Precedence: The priority of consideration of a motion.

Presiding Officer: The person in charge of running the meeting, such as a mayor, president, or CEO.

Prevailing Side: The side that has the most votes and wins.

Previous Notice: A notice that is given before the meeting stating that a motion will be discussed.

Previous Question: A motion that calls to end the current debate and to vote.

Primary Amendment: The first amendment made to a motion.

Privileged Motion: A motion that pertains to the particular rights of the members of the group overall with no relation to the pending question, but of an urgency that it takes priority over other motions.

Pro Tem: In the interim or acting temporarily, in Latin means "for the time being."

Proviso: An article of stipulation that notes a condition made to the bylaws.

Proxy Vote: A power of attorney given to a member in order for that member to vote for another one in that person's absence.

Putting the Question: When the motion is to be voted on by the group.

Q

Quasi Committee of the Whole: Means "as if in" when the entire group acts as a committee to discuss a motion. The presiding officer remains in the chair.

Question: A motion.

Question of Privilege: A question that is related to the members or the organization.

Quorum: The least number of voting members who must be present at the meeting in order for legal business to be conducted.

R

Rank: The order in which one motion gives way to another.

Ratify: A motion that substantiates an earlier action that must have action taken for it to be made legal.

Recess: A short break by the group.

Recommit: To send a motion back to the committee.

Reconsider: A motion allowing the majority to bring back an earlier motion for consideration. The only way this can be done is if one of the members who voted on the existing side makes this motion and it may not be the same day as it was passed originally.

Refer: To have a small group of members look at the motion in question.

Regular Meeting: A normal meeting of the group held at specific times throughout the month or quarter as posted. The meeting is held as often as listed necessary by the bylaws.

Renew: To have a motion discussed at a later meeting.

Report: An accounting of work done by an officer or group within the organization.

Rescind: A motion that permits the group to cancel an earlier action. This can be done with any motion that has been adopted.

Resolution: A formal written motion.

Resolve: The second half of a resolution that notes the action to be taken.

Restorative Motion: A motion that calls for the main motion to be brought back to the floor.

Revision of Bylaws: Changing the existing bylaws of an organization.

Rising Vote: A vote that requires members to stand to vote for or against a proposal or motion.

Roll-Call Vote: The name of each voting member calls his vote aloud for recording.

Ruling: The presiding officer calls a decision to be made.

S

Second: Once the first person has made a motion, it must be agreed by a second before proceeding further, or the motion fails.

Secondary Amendment: An amendment to an existing amendment.

Secondary Motion: A motion that is made while the main motion in question is still open. It is a term that can be used for subsidiary, privileged, and incidental motions.

Seriatim: Considered by paragraphs. In Latin it means "step by step."

Session: A meeting or many meetings, depending on the group or situation.

Signed Ballot: A vote that is signed in writing by the person who cast it.

Special Committee: A committee that is created for a certain reason.

Special Meeting: A meeting called at an unscheduled time for a specific reason, and only that specific business is conducted at this particular meeting.

Standing Committee: A permanent committee that is mentioned in the bylaws to perform a specific function.

Stand at Ease: A request made by the chair for those in attendance to take a moment.

Standing Rules: Rules that have to do with the administration of the group, requiring a majority vote for making changes.

Straw Poll: An informal vote to get an idea of what voters are planning on doing. This is not a good idea for formal meetings.

Subsidiary Motion: A series of motions that modify, delay or remove the main motion on the table.

Substitute: An amendment in which the resolution in its entirety, a section of, or even one paragraph or more is deleted and a second resolution, section, or paragraphs is added in its place.

Suspend the Rules: A motion that allows for the group to perform an act that goes against the rules of the organization.

Synchronous Meetings: Meetings that are held electronically with members of the group being in different locations, as opposed to asynchronous meetings.

T

Teleconferencing: Having a meeting among people who are in different locations and communicating together.

Tellers: Members who count the votes cast.

Tie Vote: When votes equal the same amount on both sides.

Two-thirds Vote: Two-thirds of the votes that are cast by members must be cast in the affirmative in order for the vote to be passed.

U

Unanimous Vote: No dissenting vote.

Undebatable Motion: A motion that is made where no discussion is allowed to be had by members.

Unfinished Business: Items from an earlier meeting that were put back on the agenda, as they were not completed in the earlier meeting.

V

Vacancy: An officer position that has no one in it and needs to be filled.

Vacate the Chair: To give up the chair for the moment so the presiding officer can be a part of the discussion.

Videoconference: The use of a television and video technology for people to interact around the world and be able to see and speak to one another simultaneously.

Voice Vote: When members say their vote aloud to be counted, viva voce.

Vote: A calling of all members to say "aye" or "no" on a particular matter on the floor.

W

With Power: A committee that is given the authority to take action in particular situations.

Withdraw a Motion: A request made by the person who made the motion to have the motion taken off the table and not considered for voting.

Write-in: A vote for a choice that is not on the official ballot.

Y

Yeas and Nays: Same as a roll-call vote when each person says their voting choice aloud.

Yield: To pass the floor to someone else once it has been given to you.

Author Biography

Rita Cook is a writer/editor who specializes in a variety of subjects, from travel to weddings, from fashion to autos, and from entertainment to business. She most recently began investigative journalism and has more than 1,000 articles to her credit from her past 10 years of full-time freelance writing. Ms. Cook is the Editor-in-Chief of *Celeb Staff Magazine* in Los Angeles and began her career in Chicago as the Editorial Director of *Insider Magazine*

while also working at the *Chicago Sun Times* for famous newspaper columnist Irv Kupcinet.

Currently, she writes full time, hosts a segment of a radio show called *The Insider Mag.com*, teaches an online travel writing class for Gotham Writer's Workshop, and is a member of the Texas Auto Writer's Association and the North Texas Film Critics Association, of which she just became president. Working in the film industry with a number of films to her credit, she also had the chance to work with Robert's Rules of Order as the President of Women in Film/ Chicago, Los Angeles' Cinewomen President, VP of Reviews for The Film Advisory Board, and Treasurer in both Los Angeles and Chicago for the National Writer's Union.

This is Ms. Cook's seventh book published and her fourth fully credited print book in addition to a romantic novel titled *Angel's Destiny*, and several non-fiction titles including *Vows and Toasts* and *Gardner's Guide to Producing Independent Films*. Ms. Cook is married and currently splits her time between Los Angeles and Dallas.

❧Index

HOW TO OPEN & OPERATE A FINANCIALLY SUCCESSFUL PERSONAL & EXECUTIVE COACHING BUSINESS

If you enjoy working with people, becoming a professional coach may be the perfect business for you. This complete manual will arm you with everything you need, including sample business forms, office plans and layouts; and dozens of other valuable, timesaving tools of the trade that no business should be without.

As a professional coach, you will recognize and define your clients' goals; construct a realistic strategy for achieving your goals; establish a detailed program of actions and activities; identify, manage, and change business improvements; get effective and timely results; monitor your progress and build on your successes; achieve what may have seemed impossible; and get the rewards and recognition you deserve. If you are investigating opportunities in this type of business, you should begin by reading this book.

ISBN-13: 978-1-60138-227-6
288 Pages • $39.95

To order call 1-800-814-1132 or visit www.atlantic-pub.com

DID YOU BORROW THIS COPY?

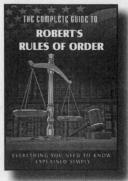

Have you been borrowing a copy of *The Complete Guide to Robert's Rules of Order Made Easy: Everything You Need to Know Explained Simply* from a friend, colleague, or library? Wouldn't you like your own copy for quick and easy reference? To order, photocopy the form below and send to:

Atlantic Publishing Company
1405 SW 6th Ave • Ocala, FL 34471-0640